Principles of Buddhism

Also by Kulananda
Teachers of Enlightenment
The Wheel of Life
Western Buddhism
Mindfulness and Money

Other books in this series
Living Together
Meditating
Ordination
Vegetarianism

Kulananda

Principles of Buddhism

WINDHORSE PUBLICATIONS

Published by Windhorse Publications
11 Park Road, Birmingham, B13 8AB, England

www.windhorsepublications.com

First published by Thorsons 1996
First Windhorse edition (revised and reset) 2003
Reprinted 2006

Printed by Cromwell Press Ltd, Trowbridge, England
Cover design Marlene Eltschig
Cover photographs (top) by Vic Burnside,
(bottom) © Clear Vision Trust Picture Archive
Photographs on pages 91 & 92 by Matt McFadden, courtesy of Bodhipaksa
Poem on p.40 from Ryokan, *One Robe, One Bowl* trans. John Stevens,
Weatherhill, New York and Tokyo 1984

British Library Cataloguing in Publication Data:
A catalogue record for this book is available from the British Library.
ISBN-10: 1 899579 59 1
ISBN-13: 9781 899579 59 4

CONTENTS

for my parents: Sydney and Edele Chaskalson

ACKNOWLEDGEMENTS

Many streams have flowed into this book. It contains nothing original. I have drawn without stint from the writings and lectures of my friends and my teacher. Andrew Skilton's *Concise History of Buddhism,* Vessantara's *Meeting the Buddhas*, and Kamalashila's *Meditation: the Buddhist Way of Tranquillity and Insight* have all been helpful, as has Stephen Batchelor's *The Awakening of the West.*

Without the writings and works of Sangharakshita, I'd have nothing worthwhile to say. If this book has any merit it is due to him. I have drawn on many of his books, particularly *The Three Jewels, Vision and Transformation, A Guide to the Buddhist Path*, and *The Ten Pillars of Buddhism.*

Sangharakshita, Kamalashila, and Nagabodhi read the manuscript and made many helpful comments. Vishvapani took on extra work in order to give me the time to write. I am grateful to them all.

About the Author

Kulananda was born Michael Chaskalson, in South Africa in 1954. He migrated to England in 1972, where he encountered the Friends of the Western Buddhist Order (FWBO) while studying philosophy at the University of East Anglia in 1976. He was ordained in 1977 and has since devoted himself to the development of the Western Buddhist Order and the FWBO, and played a key part in the development of several Buddhist Right Livelihood enterprises (including Windhorse:evolution, now perhaps the largest such business in the West), as well as several Buddhist centres. He was, for a time, secretary to Sangharakshita, the founder of the Order, and is now a member of the FWBO's Preceptors' College Council. He now spends most of his time writing, teaching, and maintaining his contacts with the Buddhist centres of which he is president.

PUBLISHER'S PREFACE

Principles of Buddhism is the fourth in our series 'Living a Buddhist Life', which examines the potential of a Buddhist lifestyle and invites those with an interest in Buddhism to explore that potential. Other titles in the series have looked at aspects of Buddhist teachings, and ways in which we choose to live our lives in the light of them. *Vegetarianism, Meditating*, and *Living Together* demonstrate that the practice of Buddhism is for the whole person, and concerns actions of body, speech, and mind.

The canon of Buddhist teachings is vast, rich, and varied, but its core principles are simple and beautiful: kindness, stillness, awareness, and simplicity. It is through living out these qualities to the best of our ability that Buddhist teachings can change our lives.

In this book Kulananda explains who the Buddha was, and examines some of the fundamental ideas and beliefs of Buddhists around the world. Ethics and the practice of meditation are especially highlighted, because it is through these we can transform our relationship to ourselves, other people, and the world.

Buddhism is proving to be of as great appeal in the West as it has in the East for over two thousand years. If we know the principles involved, our practice can start right here, right now, and make a real difference in our life.

INTRODUCTION

Over half the world's population lives in countries that have been significantly influenced by Buddhist ideas and practices, and yet, from the time of the Buddha – half a millennium before the founding of Christianity – right up until the middle part of the twentieth century, the vast majority of Westerners knew almost nothing about Buddhism. Around the middle of the twentieth century, however, this began to change and Buddhism is now growing rapidly in the West.

At a time when we are faced with a stark choice between the increasing demands of consumerism, and religions that can sometimes strain our credulity, more and more men and women are turning to Buddhism as a way to discover those human and spiritual values so lacking in the world today.

But what is Buddhism? We are used to thinking of religion as being somehow about belief in God, in one or another of his many guises. But there is no God in

Buddhism. Is it then simply a philosophy: a way of thinking about the world, or a way of leading a more ethical life? Or is it a kind of psychotherapy – a way of helping us come to terms with ourselves and with the dilemmas that life constantly throws at us? Buddhism is to some extent both of these, but it is also very much more.

Buddhism asks us to reconsider our preconceptions of what is meant by religion. It deals with truths that go entirely beyond the merely rational, unfolding a vision of reality that altogether surpasses our usual categories of thought. The Buddhist path is a way of spiritual training which leads, in time, to a direct, personal apprehension of that vision.

Every one of us has the capacity to be clearer, wiser, happier, and freer. We have the capacity to penetrate directly to the heart of reality – to come to know things as they really are. The teachings and methods of Buddhism ultimately have one goal: the full realization of that potential for ourselves.

Over the course of its long history, Buddhism spread to all the countries of Asia. Wherever it alighted, the interaction between the indigenous local culture and the newly arrived teachings of the Buddha wrought profound effects on both. In many cases Buddhism ignited a cultural renaissance. In some situations, as in Tibet, it was even the harbinger of culture. And as it moved, Buddhism also changed, constantly adapting to local cultural conditions. Thus today we have the Buddhisms of Sri Lanka, Thailand, Burma, Vietnam, Cambodia, Laos, Tibet, China, Mongolia, Russia, and Japan; and within these a bewildering variety of schools, sects, and sub-sects. Where in all this variety is Buddhism itself? What do all these different approaches have in common?

What they most have in common is their ancestral origin. They are all the different branches, leaves, and flowers which have grown out from the trunk of early Indian Buddhism. They all look back to the Buddha and they all accept and propound the Buddha's original teachings, although with very different emphases.

To understand the fundamentals of Buddhism, therefore, it is necessary to get back as close as we can to the Buddha himself. We can do this by looking into the earliest texts and seeing what they have to say to us today. This is not to reject later developments. Buddhists in the West today stand as heirs to the whole Buddhist tradition. We can admire, respect, and make practical use of elements of Japanese Sōtō Zen as much as we can elements of Tibetan Vajrayāna or Thai Theravāda, but to understand the tradition as a whole we need to go back to its roots.

Most of the basic teachings in this book go back to early Indian Buddhism. I therefore hope that there is little here with which Buddhists of different traditional allegiance would take issue. For the same reason, I've generally confined myself to the early Indian canonical languages in the few cases where I need to describe Buddhist technical terms, using either Pāli or Sanskrit as seems most appropriate.

My aim is to introduce the general reader to the broad range of the Buddhist tradition by bringing out some of its most essential (and therefore most common) elements, and to show how the fundamental teachings of Buddhism have a significance that transcends their historical origins. Above all, I want to encourage some readers to try these out for themselves. Books are very useful, but if one really wants to know what Buddhism is about one must try it out in practice. Even the most gifted writer cannot describe the flavour of an orange. Just so, no book can never capture the essence of Buddhist practice.

'Just as the great ocean has one taste,' the Buddha said, 'the taste of salt, so my teaching has one flavour, the flavour of liberation.'[1]

1

THE BUDDHA

'Buddha' is not a name, it is a title, and means 'One Who is Awake' – awake to the highest reality, to things as they really are. And one becomes a Buddha through achieving Enlightenment, a state of transcendental insight into the true nature of reality. There have been many Enlightened individuals throughout Buddhist history, but the term 'Buddha' is usually used to refer to one particular Enlightened individual, Siddhārtha Gautama, the founder of the Buddhist religion, the first person in our era to tread the path to Enlightenment.

Siddhārtha was born around 485BCE in Lumbinī, near the town of Kapilavastu, in the area below the foothills of the Himalayas which now spans the Nepalese border with India. It was a time of great political change. In the central Ganges basin, not very far to the south, powerful new monarchies were emerging which were gradually swallowing up the older, clan-based republics. One or two republics, however, still held out, and it was into one of these, the Śākya (pronounced *shark-ya*), that Siddhārtha Gautama was born.

Siddhārtha's family belonged to the warrior caste and his father was a member of the ruling oligarchy. Later tradition, knowing only the monarchies which soon usurped the earlier republics, dubbed Siddhārtha a 'prince' and his father, Suddhodana, the 'king', but whatever his correct designation, we know that Suddhodana was rich and powerful and that the young Siddhārtha led a privileged life.

At his birth a seer predicted that the young boy was destined for either political or spiritual empire (his name, Siddhārtha, means 'whose aim will be accomplished'). The legendary biographies tell that in his early life his father, wishing that his handsome and accomplished son should choose a life of political rather than spiritual empire, sought to attach him to the advantages of wealth and power by providing him with every available luxury and keeping him sheltered from the harsher facts of the world about him. He arranged for Siddhārtha's marriage to a beautiful and refined young woman, Yaśodharā, and she bore him a son, Rāhula.

But Siddhārtha began to develop an acute sense of dissatisfaction. He sensed the hollowness which underlay his superficially comfortable life, and he was unable simply to brush this feeling aside. His innate integrity wouldn't allow him to pretend that everything was as it should be. He was driven to intellectual and spiritual exploration, seeking answers that his privileged environment was unable to provide. This period of questioning is vividly expressed by the story of the four sights – four formative experiences that occurred to the young trainee-warrior while travelling about in his chariot.

The Four Sights

The story goes that at the side of the road one day he caught his first ever sight of an old man, and thus realized for the first time the inevitable fact of old age. Similarly, he was confronted in turn by disease and by death. These experiences completely overwhelmed him. What was the point of living a life of ease and luxury when old age, disease, and death were waiting in the wings – quietly biding their time before they came to claim him, his family, and his friends? Old age, disease, and death were waiting for every one of them. Finally he saw a wandering mendicant, the sight of whom sowed in his mind the seed of the possibility that there was an alternative to the passive acceptance of old age, disease, and death. But, at the same time, he saw that to embark on such a quest would require radical, and painful, action.

And so Siddhārtha passed his early years – restless, worried by matters of profound existential concern, torn between the life for which ancestry had prepared him and the religious quest towards which his restless spirit propelled him. His insight into the inevitable facts of old age, disease, and death left him with an acute and ineradicable sense of the painful vacuity of the pleasures and plottings of upper-class Śākyan life. Ancestral duty demanded that he join in, put his sense of the hollowness of things aside, and get on with the business of warriorship and government. Yet, at his core, where he was truest to himself, he knew that a life that denied the fundamentals of reality was not for him. He saw that he had two stark options: he could deny himself reality or he could deny himself family, luxury, and power. He chose to seek reality and, at the age of twenty-nine, without the approval or even knowledge of his wife or his father, he stole away from home, leaving behind wife, child, family, and social status. He cut off his hair and beard, swapped his warrior garb for the rag robes of a religious mendicant, and began his search for truth and liberation.

It was an unsettled time. Rival kings, striving to establish ever larger kingdoms, were gradually absorbing and centralizing the earlier family and tribe-oriented social structures. The old religion of the Vedas and its Brahminical priesthood was increasingly associated with these centralized governments, and a new class of religious practitioner was emerging. These were the wandering ascetics who, dissatisfied with social conventions and with the empty ritualism of established religion, gave up their homes and social positions to wander at will in the world, living on alms and seeking spiritual liberation. Siddhārtha became a 'wanderer'.

Ascetic Practices

He sought out the most famous spiritual teachers of his time, but soon surpassed them in spiritual attainment and, realizing that even the lofty heights to which they had led him didn't provide the answers he was seeking, he left each of them in turn and continued his quest alone.

In those days, it was a commonly accepted belief that one liberated the spirit by weakening the prison of the flesh, and for the next six years Siddhārtha engaged in the practice of extreme austerities. He went without clothes, didn't wash, and went without food and sleep for increasingly long periods.

> All my limbs became like knotted stalks or dead creepers, my buttocks like a bullock's hoof, my protruding backbone like a string of balls, my gaunt ribs as the rotten rafters of a collapsed shed. The pupils of my eyes appeared recessed and sunken in their sockets, like sparkling water in a deep well, and my scalp was shrivelled and shrunk as a bitter white gourd is shrivelled and shrunk by a hot wind, after being cut whilst raw. When I thought to touch the skin of my stomach, it was my backbone I took hold of, and vice versa, in so far as the one adhered to the other.… When, soothing the body, I stroked my limbs with my hand, the body hair fell out, rotten at the roots.[2]

Renowned for the extent of his asceticism, his fame 'rang like a bell' throughout northern India and he began to attract a following. But he was still not satisfied. Six years after leaving home he was no nearer to resolving the fundamental questions of existence than he had been at the beginning of his quest. Realizing that his austerities had led him nowhere, despite his great name and reputation as a holy ascetic, Siddhārtha had the moral courage to abandon his course. He began to eat in moderation and his former disciples, scandalized by this backsliding, left him in disgust.

He was now completely alone. Family, clan, reputation, followers – he abandoned them all. All his attempts to break through the veil of ignorance had failed. Desolate, he didn't know which way to turn next. Only one thing was certain – he would not abandon his quest.

At this point a memory rose to the surface of his mind. When he was quite young, sitting in the shade of a rose-apple tree, he had watched his father ploughing. Relaxed by the slow, steady rhythm of the ox-team, content in the cool shade, he had spontaneously slipped into a concentrated meditative state. Might that be the way to Enlightenment?

In this state of acute existential solitude, his determination unshaken, Siddhārtha sat down under a tree with this declaration,

> Here on this seat may my body shrivel up, my skin, my bones, my flesh may dissolve, but my body will not move from this very seat until I have obtained Enlightenment.[3]

For days and nights he sat there in meditation.

Enlightenment

The legends present a vivid account of the existential struggle that Siddhārtha was now engaged in. It was time for his confrontation with Māra, the Evil One – the archetypal embodiment of all that stands between us and the truth.

Seeing Siddhārtha sitting thus determinedly in meditation, Māra shook with fright:

> He had with him his three sons – Flurry, Gaiety, and Sullen Pride – and his three daughters – Discontent, Delight, and Thirst. These asked him why he was so disconcerted in his mind. And he replied to them with these words: 'Look over there at that sage, clad in the armour of determination, with truth and spiritual virtue as his weapons, the arrows of his intellect drawn ready to shoot! He has sat down with the firm intention of conquering my realm. No wonder that my mind is plunged in deep despondency! If he should succeed in overcoming me, and could proclaim to the world the way to final beatitude, then my realm would be empty to-day.… But so far he has not yet won the eye of full knowledge. He is still within my sphere of influence. While there is time I therefore will attempt to break his solemn purpose, and throw myself against him like the rush of a swollen river breaking against the embankment!'

> But Mara could achieve nothing against the Bodhisattva, and he and his army were defeated, and fled in all directions – their elation gone, their toil rendered fruitless, their rocks, logs, and trees scattered everywhere. They behaved

like a hostile army whose commander had been slain in battle. So Mara, defeated, ran away together with his followers. The great seer, free from the dust of passion, victorious over darkness' gloom, had vanquished him.[4]

Siddhārtha sat calmly beneath the tree, allowing his mind to become still. Gradually all the different currents of his psyche began to flow together. His concentration steadily increased. As it grew more and more focused Siddhārtha's mind became clearer and brighter. Not allowing anything to impede this process, he let it grow and strengthen. On and on, deeper and deeper into meditation, his mind became clear as a blazing diamond, glowing with ever-increasing brilliance. It was intensely pleasurable, but Siddhārtha wasn't distracted by the pleasure. Letting go of it, he entered states of increasingly profound equanimity.

The bright rays of his concentrated mind gradually began to light up the past. He remembered all the details of his past, back to his earliest childhood, and then, suddenly, he saw back even further than that, and he began to recall his previous life. As his concentration deepened he saw further and further back – an endless stream of lives, arising and passing away in unending succession. Here he had been born, with this name, lived in that way, died at such an age, and had been reborn in such a place – again and again, over and over. He saw each life in complete detail. On and on, the rhythm repeated unendingly. Birth, growth, disease, and death; birth, growth, disease, and death; an endless round.

Then the barriers that had divided him from others fell away and he saw before him the lives of countless other beings, their struggles, successes, and failures, and he felt the unfailing rhythm of their lives: birth and death, birth and death, birth and death – the timeless pulse of suffering humanity.

Siddhārtha began to discern a pattern within this ceaseless flux of change. Those whose lives had been based in kindness and generosity were reborn in happy circumstances, those who gave way to greed and hatred were inevitably reborn in states of suffering. Watching life after life he found that he could predict the outcomes of people's actions: those who spread happiness generated happy circumstances for themselves; those who caused pain and separation found themselves alone in a hostile world. It was so clear and yet, preoccupied with their petty dealings, people failed to see it.

Siddhārtha began to identify each step of the process whereby the unending stream of birth and death took place. Birth and death followed from craving. It was their deep craving for existence that led beings from life to life in an endless round of suffering. With the cessation of craving, birth and death and suffering also ceased. Having directly apprehended the link between craving and suffering, Siddhārtha could no longer be misled into believing that craving could bring happiness in its train. This brought about a dramatic change in his being. All traces of his own craving died away. Birth and death dissolved. The limited, human personality 'Siddhārtha' simply dropped away. All that was left was total,

luminous, clarity; perfect understanding; infinite freedom; and unrestricted creativity.

In the final watch of the full moon night of May,
complete Enlightenment finally dawned. Siddhārtha
Gautama became the Buddha.

> And the moon, like a maiden's gentle smile, lit up the heav-
> ens, while a rain of sweet-scented flowers, filled with mois-
> ture, fell down on the earth from above.[5]

Siddhārtha spent several weeks absorbing this profound
experience. He pondered for some time whether or not
he could make his discovery of Enlightenment known to
others. It was so subtle. To penetrate it required calm and
great concentration. People were so caught up in their
petty desires, getting and spending – so attached to family, friends, wealth, and reputation.

Then, the legend runs, a celestial being appeared and
begged him to teach, for there were some beings in the
world 'with but little dust on their eyes' who were per-
ishing for want of the teachings.[6]

With the eye of his imagination, the Buddha surveyed
all the beings in the world. He saw all living beings as a
vast bed of lotuses. Some flowers were sunk deep in the
mire, others had raised their heads to the level of the
water, and yet others had risen quite above the water;
though they had their roots in the mud they were reaching up towards the light. There *were* beings who would
understand what he had to say. The Buddha decided to
teach.

The Buddha's Teaching

Leaving the place we now know as Bodh Gaya, he walked the hundred or so miles to Sarnath, near the ancient city now known as Benares, where some of his former disciples were staying in a deer park. As he approached they looked to one another in disgust. Here was the back-slider Gautama, the former recluse. What did he want? They were certainly not going to receive him with respect. But as the Buddha approached they were so taken with his calm, radiant demeanour that they couldn't help but defer to him.

These were stubborn men. Hardened by years of asceticism, full-timers in the spiritual quest, they thought they had heard it all. But the Buddha seemed to be approaching life from an entirely new dimension. There was something inexplicably different about him. They got down to debate – tough, straight talking, going to the very heart of things. Their discussions went on for days. Every now and then someone would leave to beg alms for the others and then return to the fray. The Buddha's conviction and confidence was absolute. He had found the skilful 'middle way' to Enlightenment, a path leading between the extremes of hedonism and asceticism, nihilism and eternalism.

Finally, the ascetic Kondañña broke through. He saw what the Buddha was driving at, and not just intellectually. He had the same kind of experience as the Buddha had under the tree at Bodh Gaya. His attachment to his own limited personality dropped away and he too was now free from the bondage of craving.

The Buddha was delighted. 'Kondañña knows!' he exclaimed, 'Kondañña knows!' What the Buddha had discovered *could* be made known. If Kondañña could understand then others could too. Humanity *would* benefit from these teachings. Over the next few days the other ascetics also became Enlightened. Then a young man called Yasa came by. Engaging the Buddha in discussion, he too became convinced of the truth of the teachings and brought his family and friends along to hear them as well. In this way a new spiritual community – a *sangha* – came into being. Soon there were sixty-one Enlightened beings in the world and the Buddha sent them out to teach 'for the welfare and happiness of the many, out of compassion for the world.'[7]

For the next forty-five years the Buddha wandered around northern India, sometimes alone, sometimes accompanied by members of the growing community that was coming into being around him. As he wandered, he taught. Kings, courtesans, sweepers, and householders – all kinds of people – came to hear the Buddha teach. What he taught was the *Dharma*.

'*Dharma*' is a complex Sanskrit word. (In Pāli, the other main language of the ancient Indian Buddhist texts, it is *Dhamma*.) It can mean law, or way, or truth. Here it stands for all those teachings and practices that lead one towards Enlightenment. Over time, the Dharma that the Buddha taught came to be systematized. Repeated for hundreds of years in a purely oral tradition (writing was used mainly for business transactions, so the Buddha and his kinsmen would not have learned to write) the Dharma eventually formed the basis of an immense literary tradition, but at the start of it all there was just the Buddha, wandering about, trying to get people to see things more clearly, freely sharing his wisdom for the sake of all living beings, helping others to move towards the transcendental insight that he himself had attained.

Over the course of his life, the Buddha's fame as a teacher spread throughout northern India, an area of 50,000 square miles, encompassing seven different nations. He was known as Śākyamuni – 'the Sage of the Śākya Clan' – and there was an immense general interest in what he had to say. Enlightened at about the age of thirty-five, he lived until he was about eighty, and all those forty-five years were given over to teaching. Except in the rainy season, when he and whatever followers were with him retired into retreat, he walked the hot and dusty roads through villages and cities, living on alms, taking only what was freely offered to him, and addressing himself to all who wanted to hear what he had to say, irrespective of sex, caste, vocation, or religion. Among his followers were two of the principal kings of the region, members of most of the leading republican families, and some of the wealthiest merchants. On his travels he came into close personal contact with wandering ascetics, peasants, artisans, shop-keepers, and robbers. People of all castes poured into his sangha, where they lost their separate designations of caste and class, becoming simply 'followers of the Buddha'.

The Mustard Seed

Wherever he could, the Buddha tried to help people to
see things as they really are, responding to every situation out of the depths of his wisdom and compassion.
One day, for example, a woman called Kisā Gotamī came
to see him. Her child had died and she was distraught.
Clutching the dead baby to her breast she rushed about
looking for medicine that would restore the child to life.
Thrusting the dead child up at the Buddha, she wailed,
'Please, please, give me medicine for my baby!'

'Very well,' said the Buddha, 'but first you must bring
me a mustard seed.'

A mustard seed! How easy!

'But,' the Buddha added, 'it must come from a house
where no one has died.'

Kisā Gotamī rushed off to beg her mustard seed. She
dashed from house to house. People were very willing to
help her, but whenever she asked, 'Has anyone ever
died in this house?' the answer was the same. 'Alas, yes.
The dead are many but the living are few.'

Kisā Gotamī was utterly beside herself. Where was she
going to find the mustard seed she so badly needed? As
she passed from house to house the message gradually
began to sink in. Death comes to all. There is no getting
away from it. She laid down her dead child in the ceme-
tery and returned to the Buddha. 'I know now that I am
not alone in this great grief. Death comes to all.'

Kisā Gotamī joined the sangha and, in due course, became Enlightened.[8]

Aṅgulimāla

On another occasion the Buddha found himself in a part of the country which was being terrorized by a bandit called Aṅgulimāla – 'Finger Necklace' – who, after killing his victims, had the gruesome habit of cutting off one of their fingers and adding it to a string which he wore around his neck. His ambition was to acquire a hundred such fingers. He had ninety-eight, and was so desperate to reach his goal that he was just beginning to think that he might have to kill his old mother, who lived with him and did the cooking.

As the Buddha came to the area where Aṅgulimāla lived, the terrified villagers begged him not to go any further, for the danger was immense. But the Buddha quietly ignored their pleas and set out at a steady pace, calm and alert as ever.

Aṅgulimāla saw a figure approaching. 'Who dares to come like this into my territory, so calm and steady?' He was used to people trying to keep under cover, rushing anxiously by. 'Very well. Finger number ninety-nine coming up!' And he grabbed his sword and set off in pursuit of the Buddha. But however fast he ran he couldn't keep up with the Buddha, who was walking at his usual steady pace. This so intrigued Aṅgulimāla that he couldn't help calling out, 'Hey! Stop, monk, stop!' The Buddha turned.

'I am stopped, Aṅgulimāla. You stop too.'

'How can you lie like that? And you a holy man!' exclaimed an indignant Aṅgulimāla. 'I can't catch up with you even though I am running as fast as I can. How can you say that you are standing still?'

'I am standing still, because I am standing in Nirvāṇa,' the Buddha replied. 'You are moving, because you are going round and round on the wheel of rebirth.'

Aṅgulimāla was so moved by the Buddha's calm demeanour and compassionate attitude that he gave up violence and begged to be allowed to become one of the Buddha's followers. He joined the sangha and made rapid spiritual progress.[9]

King Bimbisāra

One day King Bimbisāra came to see the Buddha. They got into discussion and the question arose as to who was the happier, the king or the Buddha. 'Of course I'm happier,' said the king. 'I've got palaces, wives, courtiers. Wealth, armies, horses and elephants. I have power, fame – anything I want. What do you have? A robe, a begging bowl, a few scruffy followers.…'

'Tell me,' said the Buddha, 'Could you sit here for an hour, doing nothing at all, fully alert, enjoying complete happiness?'

'I suppose I could,' replied the king.

'And could you sit here for six hours? Without moving? Enjoying complete and perfect happiness?'

'Ah, that would be rather difficult,' said the king.

'And could you sit here for a day and a night, without moving, being perfectly happy, all the time?'

The king admitted that would be beyond him.

'But I can sit here for seven days and seven nights, without stirring, all the time enjoying complete and perfect happiness,' said the Buddha, 'therefore I think I am more happy than you.'[10]

And so the sangha grew and the Dharma spread far and wide. But the Buddha wasn't interested in disciples simply for the sake of a large following, nor did he want people to follow him out of blind faith. He wanted people to check out his teachings in practice, to see if they actually worked for them.

Rival teachings

A group of young men from the Kāḷāma clan once came to visit the Buddha. They were confused as to the rival claims of the different spiritual teachers of the day. They all seemed to make contradictory claims. How were they to choose between them?

The Buddha replied:

> Do not go by hearsay, nor by what is handed down by others, nor by what people say, nor by what is stated on the authority of your traditional teachings. Do not go by reasoning, nor by inferring, nor by argument as to method, nor by reflection on and approval of an opinion, nor out of respect, thinking that a recluse must be deferred to. But, Kalamas, when you know of yourselves: 'These teachings are not good: they are blameworthy: they are condemned

by the wise: these teachings, when followed out and put in practice, conduce to loss and suffering' – then reject them.[11]

So, yes, we have to refer to people wiser than ourselves. Teachings must, after all, be taught, and some 'are condemned by the wise', but nonetheless we must test everything we hear in the light of our own practice and experience. If teachings lead to happiness and gain, we can accept them. If they lead to loss and suffering, they must be rejected.

The Passing Away

Finally, at the age of eighty, his body worn out and racked with pain, the Buddha made one final teaching tour, giving all his friends and followers one final chance to ask questions about the teaching. To the last he was completely aware and concerned only for the welfare of others. A wanderer called Subhadda came to see him on his death-bed and Ānanda, the Buddha's companion, turned him away, not wanting the Buddha to be disturbed at such a time. But the Buddha insisted on talking with him, and Subhadda, soon convinced of the truth of the Dharma, joined the sangha.

Then the Buddha asked if any of the assembled sangha had any doubts or questions about his teaching. With typical thoughtfulness, he allowed that those who were too embarrassed to ask for themselves might do so through a friend. The answer was a resounding silence. The Buddha had made the Dharma perfectly clear.

Seeing this, he gave a final exhortation to his followers: 'All conditioned things are impermanent. With mindfulness, strive!' And with that he entered into a state of deep meditation and passed away.

For most of his teaching career, the Buddha was accompanied by his cousin and close friend Ānanda, who is reputed to have had a prodigious memory. All the doctrinal stories in the Buddhist scriptures are attributed to him, for apparently he remembered all the different occasions on which the Buddha taught and recounted them in full to a council of the sangha which was called after the Buddha's death, thus laying the foundations of an oral tradition which preserved the teachings until they began to be committed to writing several hundred years later.

For the last 2,500 years the Buddha's teachings have enabled countless men and women to achieve liberation – 'the heart's release'. In the deer park in Sarnath, with his former ascetic followers, the Buddha set rolling the wheel of the Dharma. Since then, it has rolled on down the centuries – through India and Sri Lanka, Burma, Thailand, Cambodia, and Laos; Nepal, Tibet, China, Vietnam, Korea, and Japan. Millions upon millions of people have been deeply affected by the teaching. Wherever it went it has wrought profound personal, social, and cultural change.

But what exactly is the Dharma? And what use can it be, a body of teaching which propounded 2,500 years ago in India?

2

THE DHARMA

After the Buddha's death his followers collated all his major teachings. In time these were set to verse, committed to memory, and passed down from generation to generation in what must be one of the most magnificent episodes of oral tradition in human history, for the 'literature' thus transmitted was immense. Similar, in its oral nature, to the Greek Homeric epics, it was much more extensive and more highly organized. When finally committed to writing, as it began to be around about the first century BCE, it eventually came to occupy what in modern terms would be a small library.

Having eventually been written down, in Pāli, Sanskrit, or other variants of Indian contemporary language, the Dharma – the teachings of the Buddha – developed and expanded. New material was brought in and a vast canonical literature comprising records of the Buddha's discourses and discussions, stories, parables, poems, and analyses gradually grew up.

Rather than a single, easily portable Bible, the Buddhist canonical literature is very extensive. It is traditionally spoken of as the *Tripiṭaka*, the three 'baskets', perhaps harking back to a time when texts were stored in that way. There is the *Sūtra Piṭaka*, the collection of discourses spoken either by the Buddha or by one or another of his Enlightened disciples; the *Vinaya Piṭaka*, which contains accounts of the development of the early sangha as well as the monastic code, and the *Abhidharma Piṭaka*: a compendium of Buddhist psychology and philosophy.

As the Buddhist tradition split into different schools, each had its own version of the *Tripiṭaka*, though there are very substantial overlaps between them. Most Sanskrit versions of the canon have been lost, and what remains is preserved mostly in Chinese, Japanese, and Tibetan translations, whereas the Pāli canon was preserved intact in the language in which it first came to be written down.

With the passing of time, the tree of the Dharma has sprouted new branches and stems as great Enlightened masters brought their own particular insights to bear on it. Apart from its existence in literary form, there are also oral lineages of Dharma transmission, from master to disciple, and even purely mental lineages, where the nature of reality is 'pointed out' in direct communication, unmediated by texts or liturgy. The Dharma can be transmitted in any way that results in people being brought closer to an understanding of ultimate truth.

One of the most common ways in which the Dharma has been transmitted is by way of the 'lists' in which

Buddhism abounds. Taken together, these form a vast interlocking matrix of both doctrine and method that contain the whole of the Dharma. Taken singly, each list contains within it the seeds of all the rest, for the Dharma is like a vast jewelled net, where every jewel in the net perfectly contains and reflects the image of every other jewel.

The list of lists is immense. There are, to name but a very few, those which between them make up the thirty-seven *bodipakkhiya-dhammas* – thirty-seven 'teachings pertaining to Enlightenment' – and these are: the four foundations of mindfulness, the four exertions, the four bases of psychic power, the five spiritual faculties, the five spiritual powers, the seven factors of Enlightenment, and the limbs of the noble eightfold path. Opaque as these will doubtless seem to the newcomer, these lists are in fact an invaluable treasury of spiritual teaching.

Perhaps the most popular of all of these teachings is that of the four noble truths and the noble eightfold path, which formed a major part of the Buddha's first ever discourse on the Dharma.

The Four Noble Truths

As we have seen, the Buddha embarked on the quest for Enlightenment because he was deeply dissatisfied. He'd seen the inevitability of suffering – that old age, disease, and death come to everyone – and he couldn't just shut his eyes and lose himself in the shallow diversions we usually employ to avoid confronting the starker realities of life.

The Buddha saw that life was marked with one universal quality: it was never entirely satisfying. The Pāli term for this quality of unsatisfactoriness is *dukkha*. Etymologically, it is sometimes linked to the idea of an ill-fitting cartwheel – something which doesn't run smoothly, which is bumpy and uncomfortable. It describes the way things never come out quite right. Our lives contain pleasure and pain, gain and loss, happiness and sadness. But what they don't contain is ultimate satisfaction. We never quite get all we're looking for. This, the Buddha saw, is the fundamental human predicament.

In addressing himself to the problem of *dukkha*, the Buddha adopted a classical ancient Indian medical formula: a disease is diagnosed, its cause is identified, a cure is determined, a remedy is prescribed. Applying this analysis to the fundamental human predicament, the Buddha arrived at the four noble truths.

The first noble truth identifies the problem. 'There is *dukkha*' – unsatisfactoriness. Because we are never satisfied, we chase after experience. Constantly seeking satisfaction from the intrinsically unsatisfying, like a hamster in a wheel, we chase round and round, getting nowhere. Gain turns to loss, happiness gives way to sadness. We always seem to think that final, complete satisfaction is just around the corner. 'If only I can do this or get that, then everything will be fine and I'll be happy ever after.' But in reality it's never like that. The wheel just keeps on turning.

The second noble truth asserts that the cause of *dukkha* is craving. We are never satisfied because we have a fundamental disposition towards craving. No matter what we get, no matter how much or how good, we always want more, or we want something else, or we want it to stop.

Between them, craving and its counterpart, aversion, set the shape and boundaries of our personality: 'I am the person who drives such and such a car, shops in such and such a place, lives in such and such a neighbourhood, wears such and such clothes.…' Thus we create our fragile identities. But the structure is unstable. Things change. Life flows on and we find ourselves caught in a remorseless process of continually having to reconstruct ourselves: 'I like this, I want that; I don't like this, I don't want that,…' over and over, unendingly. Such is the unenlightened human predicament: endless unsatisfactoriness, driven by craving.

The third noble truth asserts that with the cessation of craving unsatisfactoriness also ceases. This is what the Buddha saw on the night of his Enlightenment. Having seen so clearly that the whole of existence, the endless round of birth and death, is driven by insatiable craving, he could no longer live as if craving would ever produce the final satisfaction with which it constantly enticed. The bonds of craving dropped away, and with it all that had limited and constricted him. He was free.

The fourth noble truth asserts there is a path that leads to the cessation of craving: the noble eightfold path.

The Noble Eightfold Path

Translators usually render the Pāli word *sammā*, which is prefixed to all eight limbs or aspects of the noble eightfold path, as 'right'. But this can give the wrong impression: that there is a simple 'right' way of doing things as opposed to a 'wrong' way, and that one could easily get the path 'right' and have done with it. But the Buddhist path isn't quite so simply divided into right and wrong. It is more developmental than that, for it is a path of practice, where there is always room for improvement. Rather than 'right' we can use the word 'perfect'.

The noble eightfold path therefore consists of perfect vision, perfect emotion, perfect speech, perfect action, perfect livelihood, perfect effort, perfect awareness, and perfect *samādhi*.

The path is not traversed in simple consecutive steps. We don't start with vision, move on to emotion, then speech, action, livelihood, etc. Rather, one works in different ways on different aspects all the time. But there are various ways in which the different aspects of this path can be grouped. One of the most basic is to divide it into the path of vision and the path of transformation.

The path of vision consists of the stage of perfect vision only. It begins when we catch a first glimpse of an entirely different way of being. The path of transformation comprises the other seven aspects of the path and is the means by which we completely reorientate every facet of our being in such a way that it begins to accord with that initial vision.

Perfect Vision

The first glimmerings of perfect vision may arise spontaneously. Perhaps in a moment of inspiration we catch a glimpse of the vast interconnectedness of all living things, or at a time of bereavement we see the futility of all our 'getting and spending'. Some catch their first glimpse of it through encountering another person and seeing a particular quality in the way they live their lives.

To the extent that they have any value at all, all the great artistic, philosophical, and religious productions of mankind embody some degree of perfect vision. To some extent at least, they all communicate something of how things really are.

Over the course of its 2,500-year history Buddhism has generated a vast treasury of teachings: doctrines concerning the ultimate nature of reality and different methods for its realization. Fortunately, we don't have to master them all. All we need is what will help us to see more clearly how things really are and to act accordingly. One such teaching is that of the 'three marks of conditioned existence'.

The Three Marks of Conditioned Existence

In his teaching, the Buddha distinguished between two different states, *saṃsāra* and *nibbāna* (Pali), better known is its Sanskrit form, *nirvāṇa*. *Saṃsāra* pertains to the endless round of birth and death in which we find ourselves perpetually wandering. It is the state of unenlightened being. *Nirvāṇa*, on the other hand, is the state of complete freedom and unending spontaneous creativity that follows from the complete eradication of craving.

The nature of *saṃsāra* is that it is conditioned. How we are, what we think, what we feel, all arise in dependence upon conditions: our parents, schools, nation, and race have all conditioned us in particular ways, and we continue to be conditioned by the news we read, the state of the weather, the food we eat, and the company we keep. We each have a reactive, coin-in-the slot kind of mentality. In goes an input, out comes an output. In goes sunshine, out comes happiness; in goes rain, out comes unhappiness.

Nirvāṇa, on the other hand, which is synonymous with Enlightenment, is a state of complete, experiential insight into the conditioned nature of all phenomena. Seeing the conditioned nature of things, the Enlightened mind is not enslaved by them. The Enlightened mind is therefore completely creative, able to move in any direction at will. Whatever it does will be free, fresh, and spontaneous.

Saṃsara, or conditioned existence, has three 'marks' or characteristics. It is unsatisfactory, impermanent, and insubstantial.

That conditioned existence is unsatisfactory we dealt with at some length under the heading of the first noble truth – the truth of *dukkha*, unsatisfactoriness.

One of the main reasons conditioned existence is unsatisfactory is that it is intrinsically impermanent. Nothing ever lasts. Whatever we want, whatever we get, eventually slips from our grasp. Everything always changes. How simple it is to say this; how difficult truly to realize it. We constantly treat conditioned phenomena as if they were permanent: our friends and family will always be around, our car will never break down, our favourite sweater will never wear out. Thus deluded, we experience *dukkha*.

Because conditioned things are intrinsically impermanent, they are also insubstantial. So far we've concentrated mainly on the psychological dimension of conditioned existence – nothing lasts, so we suffer. With the idea of insubstantiality, we begin to enter the metaphysical dimension of conditionality.

Take, for example, the book you are now reading. It seems solid enough – just a normal book – but consider the conditions that went into making it. Think of the plants that were harvested, pulped, and turned into paper. Think of the sunshine that helped the plants to grow, the people who tended them (and the food they had to eat in order to function, the clothes they had to wear, the machinery they used). Think of the processes of transport involved at every stage.

And then think of me sitting here writing, my computer and printer, my food and clothing, my teacher, without whom I'd have nothing to say, my parents, without whom I'd not exist. And all their parents – way back in time.

Think of the publishers, the distributors, the book-sellers. Think of the English language, its vast history of development, and think of Pāli, Sanskrit, Tibetan, Chinese, and Japanese too. Think of the art of writing.

All of these are essential conditions that had to pre-exist in order for the book you're now reading to be what it is. If any of them were different, that book would not be what it is. In fact it wouldn't be here at all, for there is no essential 'book' that can somehow exist independently of all the myriad conditions that went into making it. All it is is a temporary coming together of a vast range of conditions. And as conditions change, so it too changes. It wears out and grows grubby, or perhaps you'll get bored and throw it away, but whatever happens to it next, it never stops changing. Eventually it will be landfill, kindling, or pulp for cardboard. There is nothing in it you can hang on to and say 'this is it, this element here, this is the book,' because we could just throw it in a fire and it would vanish in seconds. There is no fixed, final, unchanging entity that is 'the book'.

We take the label 'book' and apply it to a small temporary pattern within the infinite flux of conditions. We can use it with great accuracy for a time, to describe the particular way in which some conditions have come together. But that is all it is – a label – and we must never make the mistake of thinking that because we can use labels to denote patterns there are somehow fixed, substantial, unchanging 'things' behind each label.

Because things are impermanent and insubstantial in this way, because they are only conditioned, they are also, to use an important Mahāyāna Buddhist concept, 'empty' or 'void'. All of phenomenal existence is *śūnya*: empty. Things come together and pass away; there is no intrinsic reality behind them.

And yet, out of this changing flux of conditions, we construct for ourselves the delusion of solidity and intrinsic separation. We divide the world into subject and objects. There is 'me', a fixed, unchanging, solid ego-identity – and there is 'not me', the rest of life. We then further divide the world into things we like, which we seek to incorporate into our ego-identity to give us a sense of security, and those things we dislike, which we try to keep apart from our ego-identity at all costs, because they make us insecure. This fundamental subject –object duality is the source of all our suffering.

Clinging to a changing world of flux, looking for security in the intrinsically insecure, we experience continual disappointment. The ultimate security we seek is not available in a world founded in neurotic attachment. True security consists in learning to live without any neurotic attachments whatsoever. Such a state, however, is not one of sterile isolation from the rest of life. It is a state in which we experience our deep interconnectedness with *all* of life, where we don't try to shut some things or people out and grasp with clinging desperation to others. We let things, people, ourselves, simply be what they really are, not what we want them to be. If we can just do that, we will be free to respond to all living beings with kindness, warmth, and compassion.

We must, however, beware of treating *saṃsāra* and *nirvāṇa* as discrete opposites, for, as teachers like the great sage Nāgārjuna have pointed out, they are in fact inseparable. It is not that *nirvāṇa* is a place, as it were, a kind of Buddhist heaven, somewhere else. It is right here, right now.

To really see *saṃsāra* as *saṃsāra* is to experience *nirvāṇa*. The unconditioned acceptance of the conditioned is the unconditioned.[12]

But we tend not to accept the conditioned as conditioned. We always want to treat it as if it were unconditioned, as if it were really able to give us complete and final satisfaction, as if the things we like and the people we loved would somehow be with us for ever, as if *saṃsāra* were somehow really substantial and secure. So we don't experience the identity of *saṃsāra* and *nirvāṇa*. We remain deluded. Misguidedly clinging to *saṃsāra*, we suffer. We have a great deal of work to do before we can honestly say that we experience the identity of *saṃsāra* and *nirvāṇa*. For us, *saṃsāra* is here and *nirvāṇa* is a state beyond the horizon of our current being, at the far end of a spiritual path which we can, if we choose, begin to tread.

To see the three marks of conditioned existence for ourselves, to realize their truth, not just intellectually but from the depths of our being, allowing our behaviour to be changed by that insight, is to have a meaningful glimpse of perfect vision and to take the first step along the eightfold path.

THE PATH OF TRANSFORMATION

Perfect Emotion

We can often see the truth of something quite clearly at an intellectual level, but we have deep emotional investments which keep us from acting on them. Most smokers, for example, know quite clearly that smoking is killing them and they should quit, but at a deeper, more emotional, less conscious level they have no intention whatever of stopping. We are not moved by reason alone. Time and again we can see that in fact emotions are stronger than reason and if we want to do anything of any significance we can only do so with the full co-operation of the emotional side of our nature. For most of us, the central problem of the spiritual life is to find emotional equivalents for our intellectual understanding. For this reason, perfect emotion, *sammā-saṅkappa*, comes as the first step after perfect vision.

Saṅkappa is often translated 'resolve' or 'intention' or 'thought', but it is more like 'will'. It stands for the harmonization of the whole emotional and volitional side of our being with our vision of the true nature of existence.

Perhaps as a result of the theistic background to Western culture, we tend to think, however unconsciously, that we are somehow fixed and unable to really change: 'I am as I am. Take me or leave me.' Perhaps somewhere behind all this lurks the idea 'I am as God made me and I can't do anything about it.' Buddhism, however, suggests there is no divine plan. What we are now is the result of the conditions that have preceded us, and by changing some of the conditions in the present we can change ourselves for the future. In other words, we can consciously set out to change our emotional state for the better.

The Buddhist tradition has evolved a vast range of practices intended to generate more positive mental and emotional states. We will be looking at some of these later on, under the heading of meditation.

Perfect Speech

In the West we tend to divide the individual human being into body and mind, or perhaps body, mind, and soul. In Buddhism, however, the traditional division of a person is into body, speech, and mind.

In all of nature, speech is the sole prerogative of human beings, and human culture depends upon it. Through speech our mothers and teachers educated us, and almost all our culture depends upon one or another form of vocal or textual expression. Speech gives shape to the world we live in. In naming things we colour them in a particular way, and in expressing our thoughts and feelings we make them part of the public domain in which we move. What we express is a large part of who we are and how our world is.

It is a very useful experience to keep silent for a few days, avoiding books, television, and conversation, and to see what effect that has on our mental state. If conditions are right, as on some Buddhist retreats, most people find that sustained silence has a deeply clarifying and energizing effect. But we are rarely silent. To live in the world is to speak, and because our speech has such a profound effect upon us and the world around us, it too must be transformed in the light of our glimpse of perfect vision. Perfect speech, therefore, is speech which first of all is true.

> If you speak delusions, everything becomes a delusion;
> If you speak the truth, everything becomes the truth.
> Outside the truth there is no delusion,
> But outside delusion there is no special truth.
> Followers of the Buddha's Way!
> Why do you earnestly seek the truth in distant places?
> Look for delusion and truth in the bottom of your own hearts.[13]

To follow the path indicated by our glimpse of perfect vision means always to uphold the truth in every situation, however uncomfortable that may be.

Perfect speech also seeks to avoid creating unnecessary divisions between people; it is kindly, helpful, and harmonious. Seeing the power of speech, moreover, and seeing how much energy can be frittered away with it, perfect speech is never merely frivolous (although it can be, and often is, light-hearted, ironic, and humorous).

Perfect Action
At the stage of perfect action, the glimpse of perfect vision begins to affect our lives by impinging directly on our behaviour. Perfect action deals with the ethical dimension of life.

The Western Judaeo-Christian ethical system we have inherited is generally conceived in terms of Law. Moral rules are laid upon humanity by God, as for example when Moses ascended Mount Sinai and brought down the tablets of stone which he then presented to the Children of Israel.

As a result we tend to treat ethics as if they were moral obligations being imposed upon us by a higher authority external to ourselves. Buddhist ethics, however, is not theological but psychological. Rather than 'good' or 'bad', Buddhism speaks of actions being 'skilful' or 'unskilful', and these are determined by the quality of the mental states which gave rise to them.

Perfect vision reveals a world that is a constant flux of interconnected conditions, where all living beings are interdependent. Skilful actions, motivated by generosity, kindness, and understanding, accord with this vision of how things really are. They lead to a deepening of our experience of reality and a reduction of petty self-concern. Unskilful actions, motivated by greed, hatred, and delusion, generate suffering and isolation, cut us off from the rest of life, and reinforce the painful, constricting self-centredness from which they originated.

The Buddha never laid down a set of rules which all people had to follow. He did, however, offer sets of ethical guidelines: patterns of behaviour that are a natural expression of skilful mental states. The most common of these is the set of the five precepts, which enjoin us to refrain from killing, stealing, sexual misconduct, lying, and intoxication. We will look at these in more detail later.

Perfect Livelihood

The preceding stages of the noble eightfold path have all been concerned with how perfect vision transforms the individual human being. With perfect livelihood we are concerned with the transformation not only of the individual, but of society as well.

The world today is an increasingly large web of interconnected activity, far more complex than it was in the Buddha's day. If we walk into a dark room and turn on a light, we help to pour acid rain on to a forest somewhere, as sulphuric fumes rise from the power station that supplies us with our sixty watts. Using a car to drive to the shops, we partake in the ecological destruction of sub-Saharan Africa by sending more greenhouse gases into the atmosphere from our car's exhaust system. When we buy an ordinary white T-shirt, we help to pollute a river somewhere with bleach and quite probably help to perpetuate a system of sweat-shop labour in the factory where it was produced.

So long as we live in the industrialized world we are, from second to second almost, party to environmental destruction and economic exploitation.

At the same time people in the industrialized nations are under tremendous pressure to produce and consume. Those who have work are wealthier than ever before, but they are under constant pressure to perform and their leisure time is increasingly eroded. Alongside them, a smaller number of almost permanently unemployed people have much leisure but live in demeaning poverty. Neither of these options makes it very easy to live a life dedicated to the unfolding of the implications of that first glimpse of perfect vision.

Recognizing the intrinsically unsatisfactory nature of getting and spending, spiritually committed Buddhists have always led simple lives – consuming little, sharing wherever possible, and gaining their livelihood in ways which support their spiritual endeavours. But in today's enormously complex world we cannot think of ourselves in isolation; whatever we do impinges on others as their actions do on us. For this reason many Buddhists today see a need to work for social as well as personal change as part of their practice. This is a theme we will return to in the concluding chapter.

Perfect Effort

Bringing the whole of our lives around, so that they accord with the vision of existence revealed at the stage of perfect vision, is not an easy matter because we have such deeply ingrained habits. Nonetheless it is possible; all it takes is sustained effort.

The tradition offers another 'list' here: the four exertions. These consist of the efforts to prevent the arising of unarisen unskilful mental states, the eradication of arisen unskilful mental states, the development of unarisen skilful mental states, and maintaining the arisen skilful mental states.

1. Preventing the arising of unarisen unskilful mental states
There are six senses in the Buddhist scheme of things: the five physical senses with which we are familiar,

together with the mind, which is considered the sixth. Unskilful mental states arise when something enters the mind from our memory or one of the other five senses, and we respond to it with craving or hatred. We see something attractive in a shop window as we're passing and craving arises – we want it – and that desire takes root in our minds and grows and strengthens until it is satisfied.

To prevent this from happening we have to 'guard the gates of the senses' and be vigilant about what we let in. By becoming more conscious about the sense impressions we let into our minds and about the thoughts, feelings, and memories we entertain we can begin to discriminate between inputs that lead to skilful mental states and those that don't.

2. Eradicating arisen unskilful mental states

Here is another list. There are five hindrances to spiritual progress: neurotic craving for sense experience (which leads to things like over-eating), ill will, sloth and torpor, restlessness and anxiety, and finally neurotic doubt and indecision (in the sense of not being able to commit oneself to the good). These are the fundamental unskilful mental states that we have to eradicate.

The mind that is free from these five hindrances is like a vast, cool, clear lake. Neurotic craving, on the other hand, is like water which has had coloured dyes added to it. At first it is very colourful and fascinating. We can be entranced by the way the colours swirl around, but in time the colours all mix together into a dull brown colour. Ill will is like boiling water. The state of sloth and torpor is like a pond of water choked with weeds. That of restlessness and anxiety is like a pond of water agitated by the wind. And neurotic doubt and indecision is just like mud.

In order to counteract these hindrances, the tradition offers four 'antidotes'. First, one considers the consequences of giving in to that mental state. If you allow yourself to get angry, you might speak harshly towards someone and cause them undue pain, or you may even become violent. What pain, chaos, and confusion would result from that? Give in to greed and you just get fat. Is that what you wanted when you reached for the third slice of cake?

The second antidote is cultivation of the opposite. Every unskilful mental state has a skilful counterpart. If you feel aversion towards someone, for example, you can work on cultivating feelings of kindness towards them. There are meditation practices designed to bring these kinds of changes about, and we will look at one in particular later on.

The third antidote is to allow the unskilful mental state just to pass by without paying attention to it. Here, the mind is pictured as a clear blue sky and passing mental states are just like clouds – they drift into the mind and drift out again. By not identifying with a passing mental state, by becoming bigger than it, we can sometimes allow it simply to pass away.

The fourth antidote, and one to be used only as a last resort, is simply suppression. This is not the same as 'repression', which is unconscious and psychologically harmful, but rather with full consciousness of what one is doing one just grits one's teeth and refuses to succumb to the enticement of an unskilful mental state. This is how some people finally quit smoking, for example.

3. Developing unarisen skilful mental states
One can develop skilful mental states via the enjoyment of nature or the arts, in communication with friends, or through acts of kindness and generosity, but the principal method that Buddhists employ is the systematic practice of meditation.

Buddhist meditation aims at the complete transformation of consciousness. It is a means whereby the mind works systematically and directly upon itself to bring about desired changes in the level of consciousness. Meditation has always been a central Buddhist practice. The Buddha gained Enlightened during meditation, Buddhist iconography tends to centre on the subject, and all the great Buddhist masters have used it and taught it. There are thousands of Buddhist meditation techniques and we'll be looking at a representative sample of these in some detail in chapter 5.

4. Maintaining arisen skilful mental states
Having prevented and eradicated unskilful, or negative, mental states, and developed skilful, or positive, mental states, the essential thing is to keep making the effort. It is very easy to slip back. Regular spiritual practice of one sort or another is the only way to keep making progress

along the path. There comes a point when one has advanced so far along the path that further progress occurs naturally and spontaneously, but for the vast majority of us that point is a long way off. Until we reach it we are constantly subject to the gravitational pull of old habits and conditionings. Only regular practice – especially the practice of ethics, meditation, and reflection on the Buddha's teachings – will keep us moving forward.

Perfect Awareness

Our first glimpse of perfect vision was an instance of greater awareness, an awareness that is all too easily lost. At this stage of the path we are concerned to cultivate a higher and more continuous level of awareness.

The Pāli word *sati*, which occurs at this stage of *sammā-sati*, literally means something like 'recollection', but it is usually translated as 'mindfulness', or sometimes 'awareness'. The idea of mindfulness, or recollection, has connotations of continuity of purpose. Most of us are not particularly mindful or recollected in that sense. T.S. Eliot describes it well when he speaks of being 'distracted from distraction by distraction'.[14]

The reason for this is that most of us are not one unitary self but a loosely affiliated bundle of selves somehow getting by in the same body. Self number one, for example, may decide that she must definitely lose some weight this year. So she reads up on the latest diets and invests in a set of bathroom scales. Self number two, however, is having none of it. As soon as she gets the chance she's off to the refrigerator for another snack.

Meanwhile, self number three is wondering whether perhaps a little infidelity isn't what's really called for, to make life worth living. But self number four, which really took on board that strong Catholic conditioning, will only let that happen over their dead body! Which is probably just as well. What she really needs, to make life worth living, is to learn to meditate. That way all these different selves will get acquainted with one another, stop fighting, and start moving in the same direction.

Not only are we psychologically fragmented, from the Buddhist point of view we are more often than not nearly asleep. Preoccupied with a confused whirl of fleeting sensations, memories, feelings, thoughts, and emotions, we have only a superficial awareness of the present moment. We're often lost in a haze of preoccupation and anxiety, or we're numbed by the sheer sensory overload that comes from modern living. There are things to do, people to see, deadlines to meet. Very occasionally we may stop and look. Perhaps we're caught by the beauty of a sunset and we stop for a moment and attend to it. How different are those few moments of quiet, focused attention, a few moments of really being alive.

> Mindfulness is the Way to the Immortal, unmindfulness the way to death. Those who are mindful do not die, (whereas) the unmindful are like the dead.

> Knowing the distinction of mindfulness the spiritually mature rejoice in mindfulness and take delight in the sphere of the Noble Ones.

Absorbed in superconscious states, recollected, and ever exerting themselves, those wise ones realize Nirvāṇa, the unsurpassed security.

Whosoever is energetic, recollected, pure in conduct, considerate, self-restrained, of righteous life, and mindful, the glory of such a one waxes exceedingly.

By means of energy, mindfulness, self-restraint, and control, let the man of understanding make (for himself) an island that no flood can overwhelm.[15]

There are four principal objects in respect of which we can cultivate our awareness: ourselves, our environment, other people, and Reality.

We start with the body. It is worth stopping from time to time and checking: how aware are you of your body, right now? Do you know the position of your hands and feet? How are your trunk and head? How exactly are you breathing? Are the breaths short or long, deep or shallow? In order to develop and maintain a continuous awareness of the body and its movements we have to slow down and learn to do only one thing at a time. In that way we will not only begin to develop a more continuous sense of ourselves, but our movements will become more gracious and we will do whatever we set out to do more effectively. Doing one thing at a time, with focused attention, one can actually get far more done than if one rushes into activity in a continuous state of barely suppressed panic.

Next we come to the awareness of feelings and emotions. There is a difference between them. Feelings are simple. They are pleasant or painful, strong or weak. Emotions are generally more complex. If we meet someone we like, we experience a pleasant feeling and then a whole mixed set of emotions arises. Because our emotional lives are often quite convoluted, it's not always easy to become aware of emotions in all their depths and complexity. We can start by learning to recognize feelings as they arise, whether pleasant or painful, and by simply acknowledging our emotions as we become aware of them.

Some people today tend to disown their emotions and repress them. Others are intensely preoccupied with all the subtle nuances of emotional life. Buddhism steers a middle way between these extremes. It suggests that we take our emotional state into account, acknowledge it, and set about changing it, transforming negative emotions and developing and strengthening positive ones.

Next we come to awareness of thoughts. We very often don't know what we're thinking at any given moment. Thoughts enter the mind at random, swirl about, and then pass away again, having had very little meaningful effect. In becoming more aware of the process of thinking we make our thoughts more effective. By attending to the process of thinking we can begin to follow individual thoughts through to their conclusion and then act accordingly. Sustained, as opposed to discursive, thought is quite rare but by bringing greater attention to our thinking processes we can begin to still the constant hum of discursive mental chatter and start to use our thoughts creatively. Eventually, through practices such as meditation, we can learn to still the chattering mind altogether for a time, leaving a pure, clear awareness and radiant consciousness.

Then there is awareness of the environment. As self-awareness deepens we also start to see the things outside of us with more clarity and appreciate them with more depth – the motes of dust dancing in a ray of light, the colours and textures of a bare brick wall, birdsong, the colours of autumn leaves.

We also start to attend more closely to other people, to sense their feelings and emotions as they show them in their posture and expression, and to attend to them more closely. It is rare these days to be really listened to. Sometimes the greatest gift we can give someone is just to hear them out, with our full, undivided attention.

Finally we come to the highest level of awareness of all: awareness of Reality. To start with, we need to recognize that generally speaking we are not aware of Reality. We spend much of the time in a world of delusive projection, taking our immediate, subjective responses to things and treating them as if they were ultimately real and had an existence apart from ourselves. Projecting them on to reality, we live in worlds built from the thin fabric of our desires and aversions. When we are down the world really is a grim pit of despair; when we're happy it's a cheerful pleasure park. In order to become more aware of how things really are we can begin by sitting looser to our immediate subjective responses to things, trying to be more objective in our assessments.

We can also reflect more deeply on the truths that were revealed in our first glimpse of perfect vision, turning them over in our mind, trying to keep them present to us, allowing them to transform us at deeper and deeper levels. And we can contemplate formulations that point out the true nature of things, such as the four noble truths or the three marks of conditioned existence.

Perfect Samādhi

Samādhi literally means the state of being fixed or established. This can be understood in two ways. It can represent the fixation of the mind on a single object, as in meditative concentration, or it can represent the state of being fixed or established in ultimate reality. Used in the latter way perfect *samādhi* represents the culmination of the path, the point at which one's initial vision has been realized in full and one's whole being has been utterly and irreversibly transformed.

Traditionally, there are three *samādhis* in this higher sense of the term. Although far beyond most of us, they are worth dwelling on to some extent, as they give us a taste of the goal. These are not mutually exclusive states, rather they represent different dimensions of the one *samādhi*.

Firstly there is the imageless *samādhi*. This indicates the freedom of the state of *samādhi* from all conceptualization. It is a state of complete consciousness, fully aware at the very highest level but without a single discursive thought. Like a luminous clear blue sky without even a hint of cloud.

Then there is the directionless *samādhi*, a state of being completely at rest, with no impulse to move in any direction. It is completely poised, like a perfect sphere resting on a perfect plane. It can move anywhere but there is no impulse to move. All egotistic desire has been eliminated. It is a state of perfect spontaneity, but with no impulse to do anything.

Finally, there is the *samādhi* of emptiness. This is a state of complete realization of the ultimate nature of reality – that all things whatsoever have the same nature, and that nature is no-nature. As we read in the *Heart Sūtra*,

> Form is no other than emptiness,
> Emptiness no other than form.
> Form is only emptiness,
> Emptiness only form.
>
> Feeling, thought, and choice,
> Consciousness itself,
> Are the same as this.
>
> All things are the primal void,
> Which is not born or destroyed;
> Nor is it stained or pure,
> Nor does it wax or wane....
>
> So know that the Bodhisattva
> Holding to nothing whatever,
> But dwelling in Prajñā wisdom,
> Is freed of delusive hindrance,
> Rid of the fear bred by it,
> And reaches clearest Nirvāṇa.

All Buddhas of past and present,
Buddhas of future time,
Using this Prajñā wisdom,
Come to full and perfect vision.[16]

The eightfold path concludes here or, rather, at this point it disappears altogether, running far beyond the horizon of our current consciousness, into dimensions of ever higher freedom and creativity.

But we must beware of thinking of the eightfold path as somehow having a discrete beginning, middle, and end, as if each stage were to be traversed once and once only. Rather, the path is cumulative. With each step along the path of transformation our capacity for perfect vision deepens. The stronger our vision, the more impelled we will be to work on transforming ourselves. Sometimes we make slow, steady progress, at other times we can have quite dramatic breakthroughs. Sometimes we may even feel stuck. But as long as we keep on making the effort, progress is eventually assured.

These teachings of the four noble truths, the noble eightfold path, the three marks of conditioned existence, the intrinsic emptiness of all phenomena, the identity of *saṃsāra* and *nirvāṇa*, the five precepts, meditation, the four exertions, the five hindrances, the four antidotes, the four objects of awareness, and the three *samādhis* contain within them a lifetime's worth of practice. Although only a tiny fraction of the Buddhist teachings, they may give us some sense at least of what the Dharma is all about.

3

THE SANGHA

When the Buddha 'went forth' from home to become a wandering mendicant, he was following a practice that was fairly common at the time. Others too roamed the countryside, alone or in small groups, under the leadership of a spiritual teacher or on their own. And in gathering his first disciples together in the deer park at Sarnath the Buddha was simply doing what other spiritual teachers of the time did, for the broad community of wandering ascetics was already divided into a number of *sanghas* – religious fellowships – centred on particular teachers. Like Mahāvīra, the founder of the Jains, the Buddha would have appeared at the time to be simply another founder and head of one such sangha. Like the others, he taught a particular Dharma, and it was this, rather than their way of life, which distinguished his followers from the rest.

The Buddha and his first disciples lived a life based on the unwritten code of the broader ascetic community.

They wore robes made of cast-off rags, shaved off their hair, and spent most of the year roaming from place to place. They lived on alms and abstained from sexual intercourse, from theft, from killing, and from making false claims about their spiritual attainments. Like members of other wandering sects, they held fortnightly meetings at which they recited a *prātimokṣa* (Pāli *pāṭimokkha*), or verse summary of the special Dharma to which they adhered. One such summary has been preserved in the *Dhammapada*.

> The not doing of anything evil, undertaking to do what is (ethically) skilful, (and) complete purification of the mind – this is the ordinance of the Enlightened Ones.
>
> Patient endurance is the best form of penance. 'Nirvāṇa is the Highest,' say the Enlightened Ones. No (true) goer forth (from the household life) is he who injures another, nor is he a true ascetic who persecutes others.
>
> Not to speak evil, not to injure, to exercise restraint through the observance of the (almsman's) code of conduct, to be moderate in diet, and to occupy oneself with higher mental states – this is the ordinance of the Enlightened Ones.[17]

The Sanskrit word *sangha* has many meanings. As a common noun, it means simply a group or collection of people. In this sense it has passed into the modern Indian languages. Capitalized, however, we use it in a particularly Buddhist sense. As the third of the Three Jewels – Buddha, Dharma, and Sangha – it refers exclusively to the *āryasangha*, or 'noble sangha': all those whose spiritual attainments are such that there is no possibility of their ever falling back into the grip of *saṃsāra*.

More generally, *sangha* is used to refer to the wider Buddhist spiritual community – all those who follow the Buddha's teachings and live according to his Dharma.

Going for Refuge

As the Buddha wandered from place to place he encountered people and entered into conversation with them, and very often his words would have a tremendous impact on them. They'd speak of light having been brought where there was previously darkness, of something which had been overturned being set upright. And sometimes the effect of hearing the Dharma for the first time was so dramatic that it completely reoriented their lives, changed the way in which they saw themselves and the world, and had profound implications for how they were to live in future. And they would express this fact in these words:

Buddhaṃ saraṇaṃ gacchāmi
Dhammaṃ saraṇaṃ gacchāmi
Saṅghaṃ saraṇaṃ gacchāmi

To the Buddha for refuge I go,
To the Dharma for refuge I go,
To the Sangha for refuge I go.

In other words they committed themselves to completely reorienting their lives around the Three Jewels. They took the Buddha as their teacher and his Enlightenment as their ultimate goal; they took his Dharma as their guide; and they aspired to membership (or in some cases even proclaimed their membership) of the *āryasangha* and sought its assistance in their endeavours.

This act of 'going for refuge to the Three Jewels' is what makes one a Buddhist and, no matter how much they have diverged over the centuries, it remains common to all schools of Buddhism. The word 'refuge' can be misleading at first. Some people read it as 'escape', as if Buddhism were a form of escapism, but in fact the very opposite is true. The act of taking refuge in something is not confined to Buddhism. It is endemic to the human condition. When we go for refuge to something we put that thing in the centre of our lives and try to organize our lives around it; we use it to give sense and meaning to our lives.

We go for refuge to all sorts of things. Some people go for refuge to their careers, defining themselves in terms of their job: 'I am a school-teacher,' or 'I am a lawyer,' or 'I am a builder.' This gives them a sense of security in the face of the chaos of ordinary life, they know who they are and where they stand. Or we take refuge in a lover or spouse. We believe they will always be reliable sources of support and comfort. People also take refuge in the things they own. Their car may be a central part of their identity. The exact model and colour they choose proclaims just where they stand in the overall scheme of things.

But none of these refuges is ultimately secure. Everything mundane is subject to change. We can always lose our job. Our loved ones may cease to love us. Our car may be stolen or damaged. Eventually, like everything else, it will just fall apart. This is not to say that we have to abandon our careers, loved ones, and possessions in order to live a spiritual life (although some Buddhists do). But it does point to the inevitable insecurity of organizing one's life around things which are conditioned and therefore subject to change. The only secure refuge is Enlightenment – the Unconditioned. Placing the goal of Enlightenment in the centre of one's life, one can organize all the other elements of one's life around it.

The Growth and Development of the Sangha

Although the Buddha's first disciples were wandering mendicants like himself, householders soon wanted to join his growing sangha. Not all of these 'went forth' into homeless life, but many made considerable spiritual progress. The Pāli scriptures, for example, record the names of twenty-one fully Enlightened householders and many dozens who became at least 'stream entrants': those who have, through continuous spiritual effort, achieved a level of spiritual creativity which is irreversible and so have broken free of the gravitational pull of *saṃsāra*.

In time there arose a fourfold division within the sangha: monks and nuns (*bhikkhus* and *bhikkhuṇīs*), and laymen and laywomen. But it was still seen to be one sangha, even though its members might choose different lifestyles.

> Brethren, these four persons, who are full of wisdom and insight, are well-disciplined, learned [in the Dharma] and have reached complete righteousness, shed lustre upon the Order (of the Brotherhood). Which are the four? Brethren, the brother, the sister, the lay brother, and the lay sister, who are full of wisdom and insight, well-disciplined, and learned, and have reached complete righteousness, shed lustre upon the Order. Brethren, these four beings do indeed shed lustre upon the Order.[18]

At first, monastic ordination into the Buddha's growing spiritual community was very simple. Someone would proclaim their intention to go for refuge to the Three Jewels, and the Buddha would simply reply 'Come, bhikkhu, live the spiritual life for the utter cessation of suffering.' And the person who was thus addressed 'went forth' and became a member of the bhikkhu sangha. But some time after the Buddha's death things began to change. The community of homeless wanderers began to settle down in monasteries. The simple *prātimokṣa* evolved into a detailed code of monastic discipline which in time developed into a vast and somewhat legalistic body of work. Comprising six substantial volumes in the English translation, it governs with minute attention all the details of how monastic life should be lived. Different branches of the monastic order follow different (though very similar) sets of rules, and there came to be at least 227 rules for the monks and 311 for the nuns.

Being full-timers in the spiritual life, religious professionals as it were, the monastic order preserved and transmitted the Dharma. Quite naturally, the teachings they preserved and transmitted tended to be those of most interest to themselves. In time, the word *sangha* came to be appropriated by the monastic order to itself alone, and thus, today, in some parts of the Buddhist world, the word is taken to mean exclusively the order of monks, the bhikkhu sangha (the order of nuns having died out in places where this is the case).

This rigidity on the part of some elements within the early monastic order led, about 140 years after the Buddha's death, to the first major schism in the order. On the one side was the Sthaviravāda, or 'school of the elders' (i.e. the senior monks), according to whom Buddhism was primarily, if not exclusively, a religion for monks. They alone had the right to determine what was Buddhism and what was not and they sought to impose their version of the Buddha's teaching on the entire Buddhist community. On the other side was the Mahāsāṃghika, 'the great order'. They were the liberal party, representing all four divisions of the sangha: monks, nuns, laymen, and laywomen. They maintained that because the Dharma had been taught for the benefit of all, irrespective of socio-ecclesiastical status, the right of determining the true nature of the teachings lay with the whole Buddhist community, not with any section of it exclusively, and, in compiling a standard version of the Buddha's teaching, all surviving traditions should be taken into account, including those current among the laity.

They also felt there should be a common spiritual ideal, not a higher one for monks and nuns and a lower one for lay people. As the Mahāsāṃghika was, by all accounts, the larger party, they probably represented contemporary Buddhist thought more faithfully than the Sthaviravāda, which consisted only of some of the senior members of a particular group of monasteries.

Out of the Sthaviravāda arose a succession of schools afterwards known collectively to their opponents as the Hīnayāna or 'little way', and from the Mahāsāṃghika there sprang up various schools which gave rise to a movement calling itself the Mahāyāna, or 'great way', which sought to restate the Buddha's teachings in terms more in keeping with its original spirit.

Driven by the universalism and optimism that had given it birth, the Mahāyāna evolved for all followers of the Buddha a common spiritual ideal which derived inspiration as much from the living personal example of the Buddha as from the records of his teaching. This was the ideal of the Bodhisattva, one whose heart is set upon Enlightenment for the sake of all beings. At the same time it worked out a common path for monks and laity alike, the path of the *pāramitās* or 'perfections', the most common of which is a list of six. The Mahāyāna sought to overcome the spiritual individualism which had infected the sangha by stressing the ideal of working for the good, not only of oneself, but of all living beings. The six perfections, by means of which the aspiring Bodhisattva trains to this end, are generosity, ethics, patience, vigour, meditation, and wisdom.

By stressing the fact that all, whether monks or laymen, could become Bodhisattvas, and thus potential Buddhas, the Mahāyāna was able to lessen the tensions between the divisions of the sangha, which were now united through the pursuit of a common spiritual objective and the practice of the same, or similar, spiritual methods. Some Mahāyānists lived as monks, following a monastic code not dissimilar to that of the conservative Sthaviravāda and its various successors; others lived as householders.

Today the Sthaviravāda lives on only in the form of Theravāda Buddhism, which predominates throughout South-East Asia, while the various forms of Tibetan and Sino-Japanese Buddhism are offshoots of the Mahāyāna.

From this point onwards the more colourful and dramatic developments in Buddhism all took place within the context of the Mahāyāna; the so-called Hīnayāna schools getting on primarily with the business of preserving the Buddha's basic teachings (for which task all Buddhists should be deeply grateful), developing the *Abhidharma* – a work of monumental intellectual achievement – and elaborating on the *Vinaya* – the monastic code.

Unfolding the Riches of the Āryasangha

With the development of the Mahāyāna, the Āryasangha was enriched by the figures of Bodhisattvas, human and even supra-human beings whose lives were dedicated to the pursuit of Enlightenment, not for themselves alone but for all beings.

As the figure of the human, historical, Buddha receded in time, the focus of people's devotions shifted from the person of the Buddha to the ideal of Buddhahood itself. Buddhahood, in turn, was seen to have various different aspects, such as wisdom and compassion. Contemplated with the eye of the spiritual imagination, these different aspects in turn came to be represented as separate personifications of Buddhahood, appearing as transcendental Buddha figures – shimmering, incandescent forms, made entirely of light, emanating from the void and radiating their particular quality in all directions of space and time. Thus, for example, compassion came to be seen in the form of the Buddha Amitābha, the Buddha of eternal light, who is made entirely of warm red light, glowing like the setting sun.

In time a total of five Buddhas appeared. They manifested as a mandala, a schematic arrangement, and, as the different qualities of Buddhahood came to be seen in more detail, each of the different Buddhas developed a spiritual family, the transcendental Bodhisattvas: sons and daughters of the Buddhas lighting up the spiritual firmament with the blazing qualities of their compassionate action for the sake of all beings.

The most popular of these transcendental Bodhisattva figures is Avalokiteśvara, son of the Buddha Amitābha, and the archetype of universal compassion. Avalokiteśvara, appearing in the form of a young Indian prince, richly adorned, made entirely of bright white light, sitting in meditation posture and with four arms, represents the activity of Enlightened compassion in the world. Like the other figures in the mandala, Avalokiteśvara came to be associated with a particular mantra. Just as the figures themselves are symbols made of light, so the mantras are symbols made of sound. Avalokiteśvara's mantra – *oṃ maṇi padme hūṃ* – became enormously popular throughout the Indo-Tibetan Buddhist world as an evocation of the qualities of Enlightened compassion.

In Tibet Avalokiteśvara is known and revered as Chenrezig, and his mantra is carved or painted on rocks and stones throughout the land. As Buddhism spread to China Avalokiteśvara changed sex and became the benign and elegant white-robed Kuan Yin – the female Bodhisattva of compassion. In Japan, Kuan Yin is known as Kannon or Kanzeon. All these changes of form are most fitting for a Bodhisattva whose particular quality is to appear to beings in whatever form is most suited to their needs.

Perhaps 1,000 years after the Buddha's death, particularly in north-western India and Nepal, the Mahāyāna began to develop into Tantric, or Vajrayāna Buddhism. The Vajrayāna, or 'diamond way', works within the framework of the Mahāyāna Bodhisattva ideal. The greatest emphasis in the Vajrayāna is on magical ritual, with a central role given to meditation. It transmuted the spirits, sprites, fiends, and demons that haunted the popular imagination, 'converting' them to Buddhism, incorporating them into the five-Buddha mandala, thus further enriching the Āryasangha. In the Vajrayāna, one cultivates an attitude in which every aspect of the illusory everyday world is understood as a manifestation of Enlightened awareness.

Further Developments in the Sangha

As Zen Buddhism came to prominence in Japan from around the thirteenth century, the Āryasangha was enriched by the figure of the *roshi*: one who has experienced the chief aim of that tradition – direct penetrative insight into the true nature of reality. Technically speaking, a roshi is therefore at least a stream entrant. Whether this is true of all those who bear the title today, however, is not altogether clear. It's not at all easy to accurately judge the extent of one's own, let alone others', spiritual progress, and the mere fact of someone's being proclaimed as having achieved a certain spiritual status is no guarantee that they have done so.

In Tibet, around the same time, the *tulku* system began to develop. *Tulkus* are Bodhisattvas, either human or supra-human, reborn in human form for the sake of leading human beings to liberation. These are the so-called incarnate lamas. (*Lama* is the Tibetan equivalent of

the Sanskrit *guru*, or teacher.) The tulku system, which is
closely bound up with the Tibetan feudal system, super-
seded both the Bodhisattva and the monastic ordination,
with the tulkus becoming the chief teachers and the
sources of all spiritual (and often mundane) authority.
Tulkus are often known by the title *rimpoche* – 'greatly
precious one'. Some tulkus live as ordained monks, others marry and live as householders. Whatever their cho-
sen lifestyle, they are all deeply respected and revered by
Tibetan Buddhists.

Technically speaking, all tulkus are Bodhisattvas. That
this is true of all those who claim to be tulkus today, however, is not something that one can unequivocally assert.

In the nineteenth century, the new Meiji government
in Japan decreed that all monks should marry. Bodhisattva ordination began to replace monastic ordination,
but as this was granted only to those directly involved in
pastoral activity, it lost the unifying effect it had dis-
played in earlier times and became, in many quarters,
simply a mark of religious professionalism.

As Buddhism has come to the West, so too have all
these different manifestations of the Buddhist sangha.
One can meet Tibetan tulkus and *bhikṣus*;[19] Japanese and
American roshis; Thai, Burmese, Sri Lankan, and British
bhikkhus. As Buddhism begins to take root in the West,
new Western models of sangha are evolving in direct response to the particular conditions that prevail here.

Women in Buddhism

Taken as a whole, the Buddhist scriptures are ambiguous concerning the place of women in Buddhism. On the one hand the Buddha was unequivocal about the fact that women could gain Enlightenment, and he admitted them into the monastic order, ordaining them as bhikkhunīs – a development that was revolutionary at the time. On the other hand, we are told that he was very reluctant to ordain women, and gave way only after being begged three times to do so by Ānanda. Moreover, when he did finally admit them he gave them a set of precepts that included but exceeded all of those followed by their monastic brothers.

In the Mahāyāna scriptures there are a number of instances where the inferior nature of birth as a woman is asserted. One the other hand, in the very same body of literature there are ironic stories of young women chiding, and finally discomfiting, venerable old monks for not recognizing women's abilities to master the teachings.

The full bhikkhunī ordination lineage died out in the Theravāda. It was never successfully exported to Tibet and today it survives only in the Chinese traditions. There are women living a monastic life as *anis* among the Tibetan community or as *maejis* in Thailand, but their 'status' is seen to be considerably inferior to that of the 'fully ordained' monks who live (outwardly at least) according to the old established monastic codes, and the facilities they enjoy are meagre, to say the least.

Among Buddhist practitioners in the West, however, the picture is very different, with the vast majority of Buddhist organizations admitting women and men on a completely equal basis.

There is a move on the part of some women in the West, and increasingly in the East, to find ways of reviving the traditional bhikkhuṇī ordinations, perhaps by 'importing' into Theravāda or Tibetan Buddhism the existing Chinese ordination lineage, which is said to go back in an unbroken line all the way to the first women's ordinations at the time of the Buddha. Whether or not these lineages actually do so it is impossible to be sure, but in any event the women who wish to revive such ordination find themselves in a cleft stick. On the one hand they seek equality with their monastic brothers. To do so they wish to revive the traditional bhikkhuṇī ordination. But the traditional bhikkhuṇī ordination thus revived would unequivocally place them on a footing inferior to that of the monks. One of the rules they would have to observe, for example, asserts that any nun, 'even of 100 years' seniority' must defer at all times to the very youngest monk.

New models of ordination, where men and women are treated equally, are emerging in the Western tradition. To what extent these models will be accepted by the traditional schools it is too early to say.

Spiritual Friendship

Although periods of solitude may be helpful from time to time, Buddhism cannot be practised in complete isolation. If, however provisionally, one goes for refuge to the Three Jewels, one needs the support of others.

A sangha, or spiritual community, is made up of men and women who share a common ideal: they all go for refuge to the Three Jewels. They have come together out of a mutual concern to pursue the goal of Enlightenment – to cultivate skilful mental states and to reduce unskilful mental states. Holding their highest ideals in common, they are able to form spiritual friendships with one another. Spiritual friendship, *kalyāṇa mitratā*, is a friendship (*mitratā*) which is wholesome, beautiful, and noble (*kalyāṇa*).

There are two kinds of spiritual friendship. 'Horizontal' spiritual friendship, which pertains to people at more or less the same level of spiritual attainment, and 'vertical' spiritual friendship, which takes place between people at different stages of the path. One needs spiritual guides and one needs friends – companions who share in one's struggles and achievements.

As we have seen, the Buddha himself always went on his wanderings with a close companion. Much of the time he was accompanied by his friend and cousin Ānanda. One day, Ānanda, who had been thinking deeply about things for a while, turned to the Buddha and exclaimed:

Lord, I've been thinking; spiritual friendship is at least half of the spiritual life!

The Buddha replied:

Say not so, Ānanda, say not so. Spiritual friendship is the whole of the spiritual life![20]

There are many reasons for this. Firstly, one has to learn the path to Enlightenment in large part from others. This is how the Dharma has been preserved for the last 2,500 years. Teachers have passed their knowledge and experience on to their disciples in an unbroken chain of spiritual friendship that reaches back to the Buddha himself. Without those friendships the path to Enlightenment would have vanished in the mists of time.

Spiritual friendship also provides a context for self-transcendence, giving one an opportunity to put another's needs beyond one's own. It's easy to say that our sense of ourselves is ultimately illusory and therefore we should care for others as much as ourselves. Practising that is very much harder, but in a strong spiritual friendship it's much easier to put at least *one* person's needs above our own. That would be a very good start.

The Buddha once went to visit his cousin, the monk Anuruddha, and his two friends, who were living together at the Eastern Bamboo Park.

'I hope you all live in concord, Anuruddha, as friendly and undisputing as milk with water, viewing each other with kindly eyes.'

'Surely we do so. It is gain and good fortune for me that I am living with such companions in the Holy Life. I maintain acts, and words, and thoughts of loving-kindness towards these venerable ones, both in public and in private. I think "Why should I not set aside what I am minded to do and do only what they are minded to do?" and I act accordingly. We are different in body, Lord, but only one in mind, I think.'[21]

There is also the question of openness and communication. Many people have a private side to their lives which they are unwilling to disclose to others. They may be ashamed of certain aspects of their behaviour – either irrationally or with good reason – or there may be parts of themselves which they can't express because they themselves hardly understand them. In communication between friends these shadowy parts of the psyche become clearer and we come to a deeper understanding of ourselves. This is an important part of the process of letting go of a fixed sense of selfhood, but it can be very difficult to simply let go in the company of strangers, or those who don't share one's ideals.

It is also very easy to fool oneself in the context of spiritual practice – to let things slip and pretend to oneself that one's little (or even big) transgressions don't really matter. But when ideals are held in common they're more easily kept alive. When one falls back, a friend can lend a hand with encouragement or admonition.

The atmosphere of warmth and trust, so necessary to the functioning of any spiritual community, can come about only when there are deep, effective spiritual friendships present. This is something we especially need to develop in modern Western society, which is so marked by alienation, loneliness, and isolation.

The cultivation of effective spiritual friendships is a vital part of Buddhist practice. Without them, the ideal of sangha never becomes more than that – an ideal.

4

BUDDHIST ETHICS

Karma

As we saw earlier, the fundamental Buddhist teaching is the doctrine of conditionality. Everything arises in dependence upon conditions, nothing has a fixed and final essence. And this includes ourselves. What we are now is the result of the conditions of our past, what we become will be determined by the conditions of the present, and one of the chief determining factors in what we become is how we behave now. As we do, so we become. This fact, the Buddha saw, is what makes the spiritual life possible. By beginning to change our behaviour we begin to make ourselves differently. This is the root of all creativity. We are not doomed simply to repeat past patterns of behaviour, endlessly re-becoming the same person again and again. We can make ourselves anew. Every moment of life presents endless possibilities.

How we make ourselves, what we become, is deter-mined by the quality of our karma – our volitional actions. Often misunderstood as a form of universal divine retribution, the Buddhist law of karma simply asserts that our volitional actions have inevitabe conse-quences for us. It is just an extension of the more funda-mental doctrine of conditionality.

According to the *Visuddhimagga*, one of the earliest commentarial works, there are five distinct orders of conditionality, the five *niyamas*, an examination of which will throw some light on to the Buddhist idea of karma.

The first and most fundamental order of conditionality is the 'physical inorganic'. Under this category we find all the laws which determine the way in which matter functions at the inorganic level. This order encompasses all the laws of physics and chemistry.

The next, slightly higher level, is the 'physical organic', which encompasses all the laws of the biological sciences.

Then there is the 'psychological' level, including all the laws which govern the involuntary, instinctive opera-tions of the mind. That our hand recoils after touching a hot coal, for example, is an instance of the operation of this order of conditionality.

Next comes the karmic level, which comprises all the laws governing the way in which volitional activity affects consciousness.

Finally there is the Dharmic level. This describes what we might call 'transcendental' conditionality, a level of conditionality experienced chiefly by members of the

Āryasangha. Since this level of conditionality only affects us to the extent that we interact with such illustrious beings, and even then we will be unable to perceive it, we will say no more about it.

The first three levels of conditionality – physical inorganic, physical organic, and psychological – are familiar to us from our days in school laboratories, making explosions, racing rats through mazes, or whatever. Today we have penetrated more deeply into these areas of knowledge than ever before. But we have only a very rudimentary, even primitive, awareness of the karmic, or ethical, dimension of life. Buddhism, on the other hand, is founded, perhaps above all, on an understanding of the operation of the karmic dimension of conditionality, for it is the fact that we can change the patterns of behaviour that result in our being bound up in *saṃsāra* that lies at the very heart of Buddhism.

The fact that our behaviour conditions our being is the essence of Buddhist ethics. But it is not just what we do that matters; what is crucial is the state of mind from which we act.

Buddhist ethics is an ethics of intention. Acts themselves are neutral; what matters is the mental state, the volition, behind the act. Buddhism doesn't speak in terms of right and wrong, or good and bad. Instead it speaks in terms of skilful and unskilful intentions. Skilful volitions, founded in generosity, love, and clarity, have karmically positive outcomes: they lead one away from delusion and towards Enlightenment. Unskilful volitions, founded in greed, hatred, and spiritual ignorance, are what keep us circling in *saṃsāra*, an endless round of repetitive, habitual attachment.

Buddhism distinguishes between 'natural morality' and 'conventional morality'. Conventional morality is simply the set of rules and customs according to which any group operates. It will vary from place to place and from time to time. For example, some cultures practise polygamy, which in others is abhorrent. Christians happily eat pork, which Muslims and Jews find repugnant. Conventional morality may have arisen in response to particular social circumstances, but it has a way of lingering after the event: there are no longer grounds for not eating pork based on hygiene, but you still can't buy it in Jiddah or Jerusalem.

Natural morality is based on the facts of human psychology and the operation of the law of karma. In natural morality, acts are judged to be skilful or unskilful depending not on the views or customs of the group, but on whether or not they have spiritually beneficial outcomes. Skilful actions lead one out of *saṃsāra*, they bring about greater expansiveness, clarity, and happiness, and less egocentricity. Unskilful actions reinforce the ego-sense: they lead to constriction and attachment and bind us to *saṃsāra*. In short, acts may be judged skilful or unskilful depending on whether they lead us towards, or away from, Enlightenment.

Rebirth

Buddhism teaches that we don't always experience the results of our karma immediately – they may come to fruition much later, even in future lives. Buddhists throughout the ages have taught that the process of re-becoming applies not only to this life, where we make ourselves anew from moment to moment, but that even beyond the apparent barrier of death our habitual volitions determine the manner in which we are reborn.

Rebirth in this sense is not the same as reincarnation. It is not that a fixed, unchanging spiritual essence finds itself a new home in another body once the previous one has worn out. Rather, the continuum of change simply runs along in much the way that a flame moves through a bunch of dry twigs, passing from one twig to the next. One cannot say it is the same flame that burns in every twig; the flame never stops changing. Just so, it is not the same 'self' that is reborn.

Some Western Buddhists find the idea of rebirth hard to take and have argued that, given the lack of empirical evidence, we must necessarily remain agnostic on this issue. Others argue that, although scant, there is *some* evidence, empirical or otherwise, to support the case for rebirth.[22] They point to a variety of scientific studies of the issue: hypnotic regression, the involuntary recollection of details of past lives, near-death experiences, and the case of child prodigies such as Mozart, who composed and played music at the age of four. Some also maintain that there is more evidence (albeit slight) for a continuation of consciousness after death than there is for its cessation which, by definition, is not something that can be tested.

But whatever we may think today, for the last 2,500 years no major Buddhist teacher, however iconoclastic, has questioned the idea of rebirth. It is, and always has been, a traditional Buddhist teaching.

If we deeply examine our own experience, we see that the process of re-becoming takes place in the context of a single lifetime. In effect, we seem to die and be reborn all the time. Always becoming anew, we are never entirely the same from one day to the next. Looked at in this way, the view that the volitions which determine the way in which we re-become continue to do so after our death seems no more preposterous than the idea – which our Western conditioning leads us to take for granted – that somehow, out of nothing, consciousness comes into being for the first time somewhere between conception and birth. Although we may take this idea for granted, and even perhaps think of it as the 'scientific' view, it really is no more than a doctrine of miraculous apparition: from nothing, consciousness emerges. A miracle! Perhaps the doctrine of rebirth is not so strange after all.

Along with the idea of rebirth is a thought that is very reassuring: no spiritual effort is ever wasted. All our efforts to grow are, in a manner of speaking, conserved, and will in time bear fruit. This means that everything we do counts, and it's always worth making an effort to be skilful.

In any event, it is not absolutely necessary for someone to believe in rebirth in order to be a Buddhist, though if they did not they would have to believe it is possible to gain Enlightenment in the course of one lifetime.

The Five Precepts

The way in which we behave has karmic consequences which affect our progress along the path. But to the extent that we are unenlightened we can't always be certain that our volitions are skilful; sometimes our true motives are unknown even to ourselves. Because of this, we need ethical guidelines to follow. The list of five precepts is one such guide. It describes the way in which an Enlightened person naturally and spontaneously behaves, and, it is said, if we want to gain Enlightenment, we should seek to emulate such behaviour, for by changing our behaviour, we change our level of consciousness.

The precepts aren't rules or commandments. There is nobody watching over us to make sure we stay up to scratch. Unlike lists such as the ten commandments, they are not 'what all Buddhists have to do'. One adopts them entirely voluntarily, as training principles. Different Buddhists adopt different sets of precepts, but the five precepts, here presented in a translation from their classical Pāli form, are the most common:

> I undertake to abstain from taking life.
> I undertake to abstain from taking the not-given.
> I undertake to abstain from sexual misconduct.

I undertake to abstain from false speech.
I undertake to abstain from intoxicants.

Some Western Buddhists recite positive counterparts to these:

With deeds of loving kindness, I purify my body.
With open-handed generosity, I purify my body.
With stillness, simplicity, and contentment, I purify my body.
With truthful communication, I purify my speech.
With mindfulness clear and radiant, I purify my mind.

As guidelines for training, the precepts are the extension of the process of going for refuge to the Three Jewels into the realm of daily life. They give practical expression to one's going for refuge. It is not just that one would *like* to move towards Enlightenment; by adopting the precepts we begin to change our behaviour so that it accords with our ideals.

1. I undertake the training principle to abstain from taking life. With deeds of loving kindness, I purify my mind.
To be deprived of life is to be simultaneously deprived of everything which one holds dear. The will to live is common to all living things and to go against it is the most fundamental contradiction of the Golden Rule: do to others as you would have them do to you.

All (living beings) are terrified of punishment; all fear death. Making comparison (of others) with oneself, one should neither kill nor cause to kill.

> All (living beings) are terrified of punishment; to all, life is dear. Making comparison (of others) with oneself, one should neither kill nor cause to kill.[23]

Buddhism extends the Golden Rule beyond the exclusive domain of mankind. It respects the will to live of all sentient beings.

When we kill, or deliberately harm, another, we stop identifying with them as living beings. We see them only as objects, intrinsically separate from ourselves. This hardens the subject–object dichotomy and forces us back on ourselves in a state of painful constriction. Thus, when we kill, we not only deprive another of that which is most precious to them, we also harm ourselves. Love, the emotional identification of others with ourselves, diffuses the boundaries between us and the world leaving us with a richer, broader experience of life itself.

Those practising the precepts would not only refrain from murder and other acts of violence, they also wouldn't have abortions or counsel others to have them. They would usually practise vegetarianism, be concerned for the environment and the well-being of other species, and would not support trade in arms or any other product that harms living beings.

2. I undertake to abstain from taking the not-given. With open-handed generosity, I purify my mind.
Just as we don't want to die, so we don't want to be forcibly parted from our possessions. What we own is a major part of our ego-identity, and forcibly depriving someone of their property is a form of violence against

them. Not only should we not take another person's property, we should also not take their time or energy unless it is freely offered.

Instead of taking, we can learn to give. Our fundamental orientation is to preserve our ego-identity by incorporating into it what we think will conduce to its security and well-being. This fundamental drive, which keeps us bound up in *saṃsāra* and is the source of all our suffering, can gradually be changed through the conscious practice of generosity. Giving is the natural counterpart of non-violence and, just as the Buddhist path can be seen as a training in non-violence, it is also a training in generosity. By cultivating generosity we begin to undo the bonds of egocentricity.

3. I undertake to abstain from sexual misconduct. With stillness, simplicity, and contentment, I purify my body.
The Buddhist scriptures have very little to say on the subject of sex. Monks and nuns take a precept of chastity, and their monastic codes go into great detail about what kinds of act this precludes, but for those who are not living monastic lives not much is said. This precept is usually interpreted as implying abstention from rape, adultery, and abduction, but there is clearly more to it than that.

Sex is a very important issue for all of us. The sexual instinct is very strong, and drives us to all kinds of strange behaviour. One thing that marks Buddhist culture, however, is that it has never sought to control sexuality by means of guilt, and, if one visits some of the countries of Asia, one finds them refreshingly guilt-free.

Buddhism doesn't discriminate between people on the basis of their sexual preferences. You can be heterosexual, homosexual, onanistic, transvestite, or celibate. Nor has Buddhism ever ennobled the nuclear couple. Marriage is not a sacrament in Buddhism, it is simply a social contract, and if one looks at the various Buddhist cultures around the world one finds socially accepted instances of monogamy, polygamy, and polyandry. These are just different ways of arranging your life.

The important thing is that one doesn't harm other people by one's sexual behaviour or put a disproportionate emphasis on the value of sex itself. We live in a culture that places a massively disproportionate emphasis on sex; it is at the centre of so many people's lives. In going for refuge to the Three Jewels, however, one begins to move sex from the centre to the periphery of one's life and to decrease one's attachment to it.

The tension of sexual polarization and sexual desire hardens the subject–object duality. In a state of sexual arousal we see the person who is the object of our desire as just that, an object. For many of us, our consciousness is never so hardened into a state of anxious separateness as when we are sexually aroused, especially if our sexual desire is frustrated. The opposite of this state is contentment, being at ease with oneself and with the world, which comes about not through the satisfaction of desire but ultimately through its non-arising.

4. I undertake to refrain from false speech. With truthful communication I purify my speech.

Human culture is made up in large part from the inter-woven fabric of human communication, and for communication to be meaningful it must also be true. If we cannot have faith that what is being communicated is, in an ordinary sense, true, then society rapidly breaks down.

To lie is therefore to commit an act of violence against society. But when we lie, we also diminish ourselves. In most cases we lie in order to protect our ego-identity. In lying, we are thrust back into self-protectiveness, perpetuating a process whereby we circle within the narrow sphere of self-preoccupation.

Lying is also an act of violence against other individuals. By keeping the truth from them they are thrust into a fog of unreality. In going for refuge to the Buddha, we go for refuge to one who discovered and embodies the truth of things. The Dharma is that truth, and the Sangha is all those men and women who have made that truth their own. Untruth is the very opposite of the intentions of Buddhism as a whole.

5. I undertake to abstain from intoxicants. With mindfulness clear and radiant, I purify my mind.

Mental clarity is one of the qualities most prized in Buddhism. It is the means by which we finally penetrate the fog of delusion that is the source of universal suffering. Through clarity of mind we begin to free ourselves from the bonds of ignorance and become able to help others to do the same.

Buddhist meditation practice is centred on the development of mental and emotional clarity. It gives rise to feelings of joy and liberation as the oppressive fog of confusion begins to lift. As one becomes increasingly committed to developing and sustaining clear states of mind, one naturally becomes less inclined to sacrifice one's hard-won clarity for the sake of a few glasses of alcohol. At the same time, as one's sensitivity increases as a result of meditation practice, one becomes increasingly conscious of the toxic effects of alcohol on the system.

A modern list of intoxicants would include not only drink and drugs, but all those activities which dull, confuse, or derange the mind. It can be intoxicating to be in a crowd at a football match or a night club. Too much television numbs the mind. Even shopping can be an intoxicating habit.

The habitual use of intoxicants leads to dependence. If one takes a glass of whisky to relax every evening, eventually one can't relax without it. Through practising Buddhism, one learns in time to relax and simply enjoy one's mental states without recourse to intoxicants.

Once one has experienced the bliss of meditative absorption, the pleasures of intoxication are like cheap daubs for sale on the railings outside an art gallery. Why be distracted by these when so many treasures lie waiting within?

5

MEDITATION

We have no fixed self. Instead we're a constantly changing flux of conditions, loosely bundled together into an identifiable pattern we call 'me'. This process of change can be random: we can be blown along, reacting to circumstances as they occur, blindly responding with craving to pleasant feelings, with aversion to unpleasant ones, all the time caught up in the delusion that it will somehow be possible to get what we really want from the changing stream of circumstances and then everything will be all right, for ever. Or we can live more consciously. Having caught at least a glimpse of the delusive nature of the idea that craving and aversion can produce a final, unchanging set of circumstances, where everything will be just right for ever, we can set out to free ourselves from bondage to that delusion. By working to transform craving into generosity, aversion into compassion, and delusion into wisdom, we can begin to expand our awareness so that it no longer circles about itself, confined within the hard, cold, isolating boundaries of egocentricity.

In the previous chapter we saw how our mental states affect, and are affected by, our behaviour. In this chapter we will look at how we can change the quality of our mental states by working on them directly in meditation, and we will see how this can help us to cultivate wisdom – a direct, intuitive apprehension of the nature of reality itself.

The traditional term for meditation is *bhāvanā*: mental and emotional development. It is the systematic attempt to bring about certain desired changes in one's mental state by working directly on the mind in all its dimensions. There are a large number of different Buddhist meditation practices, but they can be broadly divided into two main categories: *samatha* and *vipassanā*.

Samatha meditations are intended to develop higher mental states – marked by integration, concentration, calm, and positive emotion – as well as states of deep meditative absorption. *Vipassanā* meditations are intended to develop insight into things as they really are.

We will look at each of these in turn, but first, a warning. You can no more learn to meditate by reading a description in a book than you can learn to drive by reading the handbook of a car. I hope to give some idea of what Buddhist meditation is about, but I am not setting out to teach meditation. There is no substitute for personal instruction from a qualified teacher.

Samatha

I remember the first time I sat down to meditate. It was chaos.

I'd have a thought about what I did the day before … then a quick thought about dinner … then a dash of anger about what someone said to me … then remember a scene from a film I saw the previous week … then notice a sense of physical discomfort in my shoulder … then have a little wave of panic about an appointment I had to remember the following day … then plan what I was going to have for breakfast … then feel a little burst of warmth for the funny guy who runs that vegetable stall on the market … then wonder whether coffee really was bad for me … then catch a random glimpse of a half-remembered scene from Paris … then wonder whether language really did delineate experience … then hope tomorrow would be sunny … then wonder about my friend … what she said … then feel irritable with my knee … all in less than five minutes.

It is quite common to have this sort of experience when first learning to meditate (that is, if you don't just fall asleep), and the really sobering realization is that this is how our minds are working all the time, not only when we stop to look at what is happening in them. They also work like this when we're not looking.

Because, as we saw earlier, we don't have a single, integrated self. Rather, we live our lives in varying degrees of dis-integration. We consist of a number of fragmentary 'selves', all vying for attention, competing for temporary control of the psychophysical organism we call our-selves. And if we want to begin to take some control over the overall direction of our lives, so that we can begin to replace unskilful volitions with skilful ones, then first of all we need to develop some rudimentary integration.

Just as different physical exercises develop the body in different ways, so different meditation techniques develop different aspects of psyche. The Mindfulness of Breathing practice develops calm and integration.

THE MINDFULNESS OF BREATHING

Like all the meditation practices I will be describing, you begin the Mindfulness of Breathing by going to a quiet spot where you won't be disturbed, and sitting in an up-right meditation posture. Most people sit on the floor, either with their buttocks on a stack of cushions about nine inches high with one foot in front of the other and with their knees touching the floor, or, if your knees don't naturally touch the floor when sitting like this, you can kneel with your knees on the floor and your buttocks supported on a low bench (six to nine inches high) or a small stack of cushions. You can, if necessary, also sit up-right on a firm chair, such as a dining chair.

With a firm base such as this, your body naturally be-comes upright and your neck and shoulders relax. Your hands lie lightly cupped, one in the other, in your lap. Your eyes can be closed or half open and your head is upright – comfortably balanced on top of the spine. This posture is poised, alert, relaxed, and energetic.

Fig. 1: Sitting with legs folded

Fig. 2: Sitting astride cushions

Fig. 3: Meditating on a chair

The Mindfulness of Breathing is divided into four stages of equal length. Most people begin by practising for ten or twenty minutes in all. Those who keep up a regular practice usually sit for forty minutes or more.

You begin by attending to the process of breathing itself. Not trying to interfere with the process; not making the breaths longer or shorter; you just attend to the process of breathing, becoming increasingly aware of it. In the first stage, to help keep your attention on the breath, just count each breath to yourself, at the end of every out-breath. Breathe in, breathe out, and count 'one'. Breathe in, breathe out, and count 'two' … and so on up to 'ten'. Then go back to 'one', and so the cycle continues, counting the out-breaths from one to ten, over and over.

In the second stage the practice becomes slightly more subtle. Rather than counting after the out-breath, you count before the in-breath, from one to ten, over and over.

In the third stage, stop counting and just watch the breath, attending to the process of breathing, just letting it flow and sitting with it, being fully attentive to it.

In the fourth stage, you focus your attention at that point where you first become aware of breath entering your body. It might be a slight tickle at the tip of the nose, inside the nose, or at the back of the throat. Wherever this sensation occurs, locate it and attend fully to it, as it changes with every passing moment.

If you can allow your attention to rest, happily and undistractedly, on such a subtle moment of experience for even only five minutes, then you will have become highly concentrated. Your energies will all be flowing together and you will be in a very relaxed and highly refined mental state.

Although this might sound simple, it can be a little difficult at first. It's quite common, for instance, to find oneself counting 'thirty-two, thirty-three, thirty-four' … having quite forgotten to return to 'one' after reaching ten. And most people find that, even if they can put aside the sheer physical discomfort of all their accumulated bodily tension, their minds just wander off on courses of their own, oblivious to any attempt to keep them focused on the breath.

But perseverance furthers. There are a number of techniques one can employ to work in meditation.[24] For example, we saw on p.44 that there are five hindrances that obstruct one's efforts to develop skilful mental states, and there are four traditional methods for eradicating these hindrances. An experienced meditation instructor will be able to help one negotiate the reefs that can wreck our attempts to gain concentration.

The rewards for persistent effort in meditation are substantial. One grows calmer, clearer, more relaxed, and more directed in one's intentions. One may also experience the pleasures of the *dhyānas* – superconscious states of meditative absorption.

THE DHYĀNAS

As we saw earlier, we don't have a single, unitary self. We're just a loose bundle of selves tied together by a vague sense of self-identity, and these selves are often in a state of conflict with one another. In order to progress along the spiritual path we need to bring these different selves together into a more harmonious, integrated, whole. We can integrate ourselves 'horizontally', at the psychological level of being, getting our different selves to become aware of one another and encouraging them to co-operate, and we can integrate ourselves 'vertically', by experiencing the heights and depths of our more 'spiritual' potential.

There are four *dhyānas*, each successively more refined. The first two pertain to the dimension of horizontal, or psychological, integration. The other two, in which one's experience is less divided into experiencing subject and experienced object, pertain to vertical integration.

The *dhyānas* don't arise in dependence upon anything external to us. They are states of extreme blissful happiness which are the psychophysical reflex of deep absorption. The first *dhyāna* is a state of integration characterized by an absence of the hindrances, all one's previously conflicting psychophysical energies having come to a state of at least temporary unification. One is simply happy being who one is and doing what one is doing. There is still a certain amount of mental activity present, but it doesn't distract from the meditation and one just sits, happy and contented, maybe feeling an occasional shudder of rapture.

If one can stay with that state, without falling into distraction, then discursive thinking begins to die away, rapture calms down, one becomes even more aware and alert, and moves into the second *dhyāna*.

This is the state of inspiration. Here, the mind becomes like a vast clear lake of sparkling pure water, calm and tranquil, and, as if from nowhere, a spring of fresh water, of inspiration, bubbles up into the lake, feeding and expanding it. It is a state of intense delight. If one stays relaxed, clear, undistracted, and receptive to the very subtle movements and changes that are now taking place in one's mind, the water from the lake can, as it were, overflow its banks and one moves into the third *dhyāna*.

Here the boundaries of the psychophysical organism have become highly attenuated. One hardly experiences oneself as having a body at all. Fully absorbed in meditation, one begins to have a first taste of the blissful possibilities of radiant limitlessness.

Entering the fourth *dhyāna*, even bliss dies away. Subjectivity itself has become almost completely attenuated. There is just the intense radiance of a state of equanimity, even more pleasurable than pleasure. It is a state of perfect harmony and equilibrium.

Such are the heights of *samatha*. With a mind clarified, refreshed, and made pliable by experiences like these, one can begin to contemplate the nature of reality and see it in its depths, unmediated by distracting subjectivity. Such heights are not easy to scale, but others have gone before us, the *dhyānas* can be attained, and, given a little time and supportive conditions, most people can quite easily gain some experience of at least the first two.

One of the factors that prevent us experiencing the *dhyānas* spontaneously is our tendency towards habitual negative emotions: craving, anger, irritability, jealousy, and so on. The *mettā bhāvanā* is a meditation practice designed to transform these. In particular, it develops our capacity for *mettā* – loving kindness.

METTĀ BHĀVANĀ

Bhāvanā, as we have seen, means 'development' and is a synonym for meditation, but there isn't a satisfactory translation for the word *mettā*. It means something like 'loving-kindness', but that can easily be associated with sentimentality. One could use the word 'love', but that has come to have connotations of exclusivity and neurotic attachment. *Mettā*, on the other hand, is a feeling of universal, all-pervading, well-wishing. It is a broad, inclusive state of warm, intense good-will.

The practice is divided into five stages of more or less equal length. In the first stage you try to cultivate feelings of *mettā* towards yourself. There are various techniques you can use to do this and personal meditation instruction is the best way to learn these.

In the first stage you simply try to contact feelings of warmth, goodwill, kindness, and well-wishing towards yourself. You don't merely think about feelings of *mettā* in this practice, you try to feel them in your heart, rather than in your head.

In the second stage you call to mind a friend, someone who is not a sexual partner, and of a similar age to yourself (otherwise your feelings of *mettā* may be confused with parental, filial, or sexual feelings). Bearing this friend in mind, you try to develop ever stronger feelings of *mettā* towards them.

In the third stage, call to mind a 'neutral' person, someone with whom you have fairly regular contact but for whom you don't feel any strong feelings one way or the other. Trying to get a sense of their humanity, you cultivate feelings of *mettā* towards them.

In the fourth stage, you call to mind an enemy, or someone with whom your communication is a little abrasive, or with whom communication has broken down, and try to develop feelings of *mettā* towards them.

In the fifth and final stage you bring to mind all four people: yourself, your friend, the neutral person, and the enemy, and cultivate feelings of warmth and *mettā* for all four, equally and impartially. From there, you begin to radiate that feeling of *mettā* outwards. Beginning with everyone in your immediate vicinity, then reaching out into the neighbourhood, the town, the county, the country, the continent, the world – radiating feelings of warmth and *mettā* to all beings everywhere.

The *mettā bhāvanā* is a powerfully transforming practice. Once they have a little experience of it, most people find they can use it almost without fail to bring about an improvement in their mental state. With regular practice you will come to develop deep reserves of *mettā* that you can call upon more or less at will.

Vipassanā

However refined, however strong, the states of *samatha* you cultivate might be, they are nonetheless still subject to mundane conditions. When the conditions that gave rise to them pass, they melt away like the morning dew. The only way to escape from the gravitational pull of mundane conditions is by the development of *vipassanā*: direct, experiential insight into the nature of things as they really are.

There are a number of practices designed to generate such insight, but they all require a substantial grounding in *samatha* in order to be effective. Unless you are sufficiently integrated, you will not be able to bring your whole being to *vipassanā* practice. Without that integration, *vipassanā* practices might be useful to some extent, but they won't be irreversibly transformative. And unless you have developed a high level of positive emotion, the existential shock that *vipassanā* practice can produce might throw you seriously off course, for the intention of *vipassanā* is to bring about the direct experience of *śūnyatā*: emptiness. *Vipassanā* practices are designed to enable us to penetrate the myth of substantiality and experience for ourselves directly the unsatisfactory, impermanent, and insubstantial nature of all phenomena – thus freeing us, once and for all, from bondage to *saṃsāra*. One such practice is the contemplation of the six elements.

THE SIX ELEMENT PRACTICE

According to Indian tradition, the material world is made up of four great elements: earth, water, fire, and air. All material objects, including our bodies, can be reduced to these elements. When we add to these the elements of space and consciousness they give us, in ascending order of refinement, a complete description of the make-up of the whole psychophysical organism. Apart from these elements there is no 'self'; we construct our fixed sense of ourselves from the six elements. If we want to free ourselves from that delusion and experientially apprehend the true nature of things, we must let go of our attachment to the six elements altogether. That is what one sets out to do in this meditation.

You start by establishing a foundation of mindfulness and emotional positivity, and then you begin with the earth element. You reflect that everything in yourself that is hard and solid, everything that offers resistance – bones, hair, skin, and teeth – all these are just part of the great earth element in the universe. You can't hold on to them for ever. When you die, they will return to the earth. You have only borrowed them, they are not 'you', and you shouldn't identify with them. Since they are not 'yours' you might as well allow them to return to the great earth element in the universe. And so you imaginatively let go of all the manifestations of the earth element in your body. You cease to cling to them, cease to identify yourself with them. You let them go, and feel a consequent lightening and sense of liberation.

Going on to the water element, you consider that, in part, you are made of water. All the fluids in your body are just various transformations of the water element. But these fluids don't really belong to you, you can't hold on to them for ever, you have borrowed them from the great water element in the universe and when you die they will return to that great water element. Blood, tears, perspiration, urine – none of your bodily fluids have any permanence, none of them are finally your own. So, again, you give them up. Allow them simply to be part of the great water element in the universe. They are not 'you'.

You move on to the fire element and feelings of physical warmth. When you die, your corpse almost immediately becomes cold. This warmth you now feel is not 'yours', it is temporary, you only have it on loan, for only a short while. So you let go of it, stop feeling attached to it, stop allowing it to establish one of the boundaries of your being.

Next, you reflect on the air element. You breathe in and breathe out but you can never hold on to the air in your body, it is in constant motion. It is simply the great air element in the universe which you use for a very short while. So give it up. Let go. And by now your sense of yourself has become highly refined and attenuated. You don't identify yourself with your body in the way you usually do. Although you continue to experience the body, you're no longer so attached to that experience and there is a more refined quality to your experience.

Next you reflect on the element of space. The space you occupy is always changing. When all the material elements have been let go, what space do you occupy? This shape you have is not 'you', it is merely an appearance created by the temporary coming together of the material elements. When you let go of them you also let go of your shape, it just becomes part of the space of the universe.

By now you experience very little sense of limit. You reflect that your consciousness is not fixed and finite. If you don't 'own' your body, how can it be the final location of your consciousness? Where *are* the boundaries of your consciousness? What makes it 'yours'? You have no fixed and final self at all. So just let go of the discursive process of self-identification, and you experience … well, you experience what you experience. At this stage we have gone completely beyond the possibilities of linguistic expression. Of its very nature, one cannot describe such an experience. It is beyond all limiting conceptions.

VISUALIZATION

Another approach to *vipassanā* is the practice of visualization. There are a large number of these, one of the most popular being the visualization of one or another of the archetypal Buddha or Bodhisattva forms.

Here you begin as before, establishing mindfulness and positivity. Then you visualize in front of you a clear blue sky extending in all directions. Then within the sky you conjure up the image of one or another of the transcendental Buddha or Bodhisattva forms who are made entirely of light, like a rainbow. You contemplate the image for a time, and perhaps recite devotional verses or the mantra associated with that Buddha or Bodhisattva, and receives blessings from them, and then you resolve the image back into the blue sky. At this point one can reflect that just as the visualized image appears from emptiness and returns to emptiness, so too do we and all phenomena.

There are an enormous number of variations on this type of meditation, but tradition asserts that they cannot be effectively practised without one's first having been initiated into such a practice in the context of a teacher–disciple relationship. Only then will the essence of the practice be communicated.

Like all *vipassanā* practices, visualization is not for the spiritual dilettante. It is a means of beginning to contact other dimensions of reality, a process which should not be trifled with. Ideally, you should avoid these levels of practice until such time as your going for refuge has become truly effective, and you can practise them within the context of a supportive spiritual community.

Formless Meditations

So far we have looked mainly at meditation practices that have a particular object and a certain amount of structure. There are also, however, practices that have very little structure and no particular object.

A large number of different formless meditations are taught in the different Buddhist traditions – *dzogchen, mahāmudrā, zazen*, to name but a few. Perhaps we are most familiar with the term zazen, which comes from the Zen tradition. (The other two are Tibetan.) There is very little one can say about these. With dzogchen, it is said, one simply enters into an unmediated experience of the innate purity of mind. Mahāmudrā is the 'effortless experience of emptiness', and zazen is 'just sitting'.

But don't get the impression that because these are formless they are therefore easy. Progress in formless meditation takes years of regular, dedicated effort, for formless meditation is not just sitting and drifting.

Here, Yasutani Roshi communicates something of the relaxed but focused intensity of the mind of one properly engaged in 'just sitting'.

It is the mind of somebody facing death. Let us imagine
that you are engaged in a duel of swordsmanship of the

kind that used to take place in ancient Japan. As you face your opponent you are unceasingly watchful, set, ready. Were you to relax your vigilance even momentarily, you would be cut down instantly. A crowd gathers to see the fight. Since you are not blind you see them from the corner of your eye, and since you are not deaf you hear them. But not for an instant is your mind captured by these sense impressions.[25]

Devotion and Ritual

Another highly effective way of working to bring about changes in your state of mind is through ritual and devotion. All schools of Buddhism engage in these activities: bowing before shrines and images of the Buddha; making offerings of flowers, lights, and incense; and chanting devotional verses. From the exquisitely formalized rituals of Zen to the imaginative abundance of Tibetan tantra, Buddhists over the centuries have devised a variety of ways of engaging their emotion and imagination in the process of transformation.

There are several dimensions to this. To begin with, you can achieve very little, in any field of endeavour, unless you have devotion. Successful artists are devoted to their art, athletes to their sport, teachers to their pupils. Without emotional engagement their achievements will never be more than mediocre. In the same way, unless you are devoted to the Three Jewels, imaginatively engaged with them and serious about spiritual progress, you will never really get anywhere. Buddhist rituals are designed to bring about that quality of engagement.

As you begin to practise, and as the Dharma begins to affect your life for the better, you start to feel deep gratitude to the Buddha for having made the Dharma available. You feel reverence for the Dharma, which is having such profound effects in your life. And you feel gratitude to the Āryasangha for keeping the Dharma alive. Devotional practice is a way of expressing this gratitude.

It is also a means of self-transcendence. Imaginatively engaging with the heights and depths of Enlightenment, you leave your petty, limiting concerns behind for a time and participate, at least to some extent, in a drama of cosmic dimensions.

Buddhist ritual is rich in symbolic significance. Participating in it you start to become attuned to symbolism itself. The effect of this is to enrich your sensibility, heighten your aesthetic awareness, and open up to the poetry inherent in every moment of existence.

6

THE SPREAD AND DEVELOPMENT
OF BUDDHISM

The Emperor Aśoka, who reigned from about 269 to 232 BCE, ruled the Mauryan kingdom of northern India and did much to consolidate the position of Buddhism. A gifted ruler, he began his imperial career with extensive territorial ambitions, but a costly victory, where many on both sides lost their lives, brought him to an acute psychological crisis which resulted in his embracing Buddhism. He began a 'reign of the Dharma', undertaking journeys throughout his realm to establish virtue. He propagated pacifism and vegetarianism, and banned animal sacrifice.

Aśoka sent Buddhist missions to the Greek kingdoms, but there is no record of their having been received. He had more success in Sri Lanka, sending his son Mahinda there as a Buddhist missionary in the first known instance of the Dharma spreading overseas.

Three more centuries were to elapse before Buddhism finally penetrated the entire Indian subcontinent. It then began to expand into Greater Asia. From Gandhara, an Indo-Greek kingdom to the north-west of India, Buddhism gradually filtered into Central Asia and from there it followed the Silk Road into China, where the first established Buddhist community we know of emerged around 150CE. Buddhism gradually spread throughout China, increasing in strength and influence until, under the Tang dynasty (618–907CE), it entered a golden age. Truly Chinese forms of Buddhism: Avataṃsaka, T'ien t'ai, Pure Land, and Ch'an all began to emerge in this period. As Chinese civilization spread so too did Buddhism, entering Vietnam, Korea, and Japan around the sixth century.

Some time around the seventh century, Buddhism was introduced into Tibet from the Swat valley to the west and from India to the south, but it was another 200 years before it began to establish itself, eventually giving rise to perhaps the most spiritually creative culture the world has ever seen.

In Sri Lanka, Mahinda's mission in the second century BCE had been successful and Buddhism has existed on the island, though often very precariously, from then until the present day. For many years Theravāda, Mahāyāna, and Vajrayāna Buddhism all exerted an influence as royal patronage swayed now this way, now that. Finally, in the twelfth century, the other forms were suppressed and the Theravāda became dominant.

Although the countries of South-east Asia had to some extent come under the influence of Mahāyāna Buddhism, spread from India or China, missions from Sri Lanka eventually helped to establish Theravāda Buddhism in the region and it is now the predominant form of Buddhism in Burma, Thailand, Cambodia, and Laos.

In the thirteenth century Buddhism began to die out in India, partly as a result of the Muslim invasion. With a fanatical hatred of what appeared to them to be 'idolatry', the Muslim conquerors burned down monasteries, libraries, and universities, and killed large numbers of monks. The pacific Buddhist monks offered little resistance and, with the destruction of the Buddhist centres of monastic training, Brahmanism, which had to a large extent already absorbed Mahāyāna Buddhist concepts and imagery, now began to absorb popular Buddhism itself. Seven centuries were to elapse before Buddhism began to revive in India.

Buddhism Today

The technological age has dawned very rapidly for most Buddhist cultures. Before the 1950s Tibet was to all intents and purposes a medieval feudal society, with most of its inhabitants living in ignorance of such phenomena as cars and radios. Most other Asian countries were still largely agrarian and Buddhists of different nationalities were only very dimly aware of one another's existence. The globalization we take for granted today has only emerged in the last few decades and the situation that now prevails all around the world is almost unrecognizable compared with what we would have found as little as fifty years ago.

Japan

In Japan, the periods of instability and change that followed World War II saw the development of hundreds of so-called new religions. Sometimes comprising no more than a few hundred people, several of these derived their beliefs from one or another reading of the traditional Buddhist scriptures. A few of the new religions have grown to be very large indeed: Rissho Kosei-kai and Soka Gakkai International (SGI), for example, number their followers in millions. Both these organizations are offshoots of Nichiren Buddhism, which traces its ancestry back to the militant thirteenth-century figure of Nichiren. For him, as for his present-day followers, the quintessence of the Dharma is contained in the *gohonzon*, which is praised with a mantra-like chant, *nam-myoho-renge-kyo*, ('Homage to the mystic law of the Lotus Sūtra'), the chanting of which, Soka Gakkai say, brings all boons, both spiritual and material.

Perhaps because of the ease and simplicity of this teaching, Nichiren Buddhism, in the form of Soka Gakkai International, has attracted an enormous following both in Japan and without, where it is best known for its celebrity followers: the singers Tina Turner and Boy

George, the Italian footballer Roberto Baggio, as well as many minor celebrities from the world of fashion and the media. It is not clear to what extent they are aware of Nichiren's own extraordinary militancy. 'All the [Pure Land] and Zen temples … should be burned to the ground and their priests taken to Yui beach to have their heads cut off!'[26] he once advised a Japanese court.

While the new religions have grown and expanded, the twentieth century has not treated the more traditional forms of Japanese Buddhism very kindly. The war left the already struggling monasteries with very few financial resources following General MacArthur's land reform and, with the economic reconstruction of the country, materialism flourishes as never before. Loyalty to a single religion, moreover, has never played a major part in the Japanese cultural make-up and Buddhism, which thus coexists in modern national life with Shinto and Christianity, is confined in great part to the conduct of rites of passage, especially funerals.

With Buddhism in decline in Japan a small handful of roshis began to consider the necessity to spread the Japanese Zen approach beyond the borders that had confined it for eight centuries. Nyogen Senzaki, Sokei-an Sasaki, Nakagawa Soen, Haku'un Yasutani, Sunyru Suzuki, Taisan Shimano Eido, and Taizan Maezumi between them played an enormous part in establishing Zen Buddhism in America and, to a lesser extent, in Europe.

Japanese Pure Land Buddhism has also made its way to the United States, where the Buddhist Churches of

America mainly serve the needs of the Japanese ethnic population.

Indo-China

In Korea, Zen Buddhism thrives under the name of Son, but it is subject to the encroachment of aggressive Christian missionary activity and, as in Hong Kong, Taiwan, Thailand, Singapore, and Malaysia, to a burgeoning consumerism fed by the South-east Asian 'economic miracle'. Korean Zen, however, has come to the West, particularly in the shape of the Kwan Um Zen school, which was founded by Seung Sahn Sunim in 1983 and which is adapted to the needs of Westerners.

In Vietnam, Cambodia, and Laos, war shattered what were once thriving Buddhist cultures. Nothing illustrates this more vividly than the pictures of calm Buddhist monks and nuns driven to the desperate act of self-immolation to draw the world's attention to the oppression which Buddhism suffered at the hands of the South Vietnamese Roman Catholic dictator Ngo Dinh Diem in 1963.

Three years later, the Vietnamese Zen master Thich Nhat Hanh journeyed to Europe and America to try to communicate the effect the war in Vietnam was having on ordinary people and to promote the cause of peace. Since those days Nhat Hanh has largely remained in the West, where he has been a tireless activist for peace, teaching an approach to Buddhism that emphasizes social responsibility and pacifism based on the practice of mindful awareness.

China and Tibet

In China, the Cultural Revolution dealt a near-fatal blow to a Buddhism which had already been weakened by centuries of political turmoil. As in Japan, the Chinese have rarely been loyal to one religion alone and today what remnants of Buddhism there are among the Chinese populations of Asia are often found intermingled with elements of Confucianism, Taoism, and local animism. Even so, a variety of more 'orthodox' Chinese Buddhist institutions continue to thrive, particularly in Taiwan and the United States. Ch'an Buddhism has also found its way to the West, but as yet it is not as popular as Zen.

In Inner Mongolia, a part of China, Buddhism experienced the same fate as in China itself, while in Outer Mongolia, for many years part of the former USSR, it suffered tremendous depredations at the hands of Josef Stalin and his successors.

Of all the Buddhist countries which have suffered at the hands of oppressive regimes over the past hundred years, none has caught the popular imagination as much as Tibet, which the Western imagination conceives as 'a land so close to the sky that the natural inclination of her people is to pray,' 'a high place of crystalline purity, sacred mystery, worldly innocence, and spiritual mastery', 'a utopia, a Shangri-la, a lost horizon'.[27]

Although this portrayal ignores the dark underside of Tibetan feudal life, where the struggle for temporal power was necessarily inseparable from many aspects of institutionalized religious life, Tibet was nonetheless a thriving Buddhocracy before the brutal Chinese invasion of 1959. Perhaps more than any other culture in history, life in the country was informed by truly spiritual values and in consequence it produced a large number of highly attained spiritual adepts.

The Chinese, however, have treated Tibetan culture and religion with a cruel, oppressive disdain, destroying monasteries and killing or imprisoning monks and nuns. In 1959 the Dalai Lama fled into exile in India where many thousands of Tibetans have since joined him. With irrepressible optimism and cheerfulness, Tibetan Buddhism lives on today in thriving Tibetan refugee communities in India, especially around Dharamsala, where the Dalai Lama himself is based, and the great monastic institutions of Tibet have been reconstructed in exile, albeit in a much reduced form. Tibetan-style Buddhism also continues to flourish to some extent in Nepal, as well as in Sikkim, Bhutan, and Ladakh.

Although emphatically not the Buddhist equivalent of the pope, as he is sometimes mistakenly thought to be, the Dalai Lama occupies a unique position in the Tibetan Buddhist world. His previous incarnations have ruled Tibet since the seventeenth century, and the current Dalai Lama, the fourteenth in succession, is effectively a head of state in exile. At the same time he is a highly qualified lama of the Gelug tradition and is thus called upon to bridge two worlds, the sacred and the secular; a task he appears to perform with ease.

The Dalai Lama is regarded by the Tibetan people with an awed affection, an attitude they share with some of his followers in the West. For although he likes to call himself 'a simple Tibetan monk', he has proved to be much more than that. As a tireless campaigner on behalf of the Tibetan people and for peace in general, he has gained a reputation for wisdom and integrity that few other modern statesmen share.

One of the positive effects of this Tibetan diaspora has been the spread of the Tibetan approach to Buddhism beyond the Himalayan region which had confined it for over a thousand years. There are now Tibetan Buddhist centres of all the major schools in most countries of the West, and the spiritual riches that had been cultivated in a state of pristine isolation are at last being shared.

Burma

Burmese Buddhism, which came to be associated with Burmese nationalism in opposition to British imperial rule, today finds itself forced into compromise with the State Law and Order Restoration Committee, or SLORC, which currently rules the country. The SLORC brooks no opposition, and expects, if not support, then at least passivity from the local Theravādin bhikkhu sangha. At times some monks have registered their protest at being expected to turn a blind eye to acts of genocide among the hill tribes, and other forms of institutional oppression, but they have been harshly dealt with.

Before the advent of SLORC, however, a few Burmese meditation masters, principally Mahasi Sayadaw and U Ba Khin, were partly responsible for the beginnings of a revival of the practice of meditation in the Theravādin Buddhist world. Their predominantly Western lay disciples now teach meditation throughout the world, particularly under the auspices of the Insight Meditation Society, which is based in the United States.

In Thailand and Sri Lanka, too, there is a strong connection between Buddhism and the state, and whereas this is largely ceremonial in Thailand, Sri Lanka has lately been subject to outbreaks of Buddhist religionationalism as the minority Tamil Hindus have fought for greater rights and recognition. The involvement of some Buddhist monks in the violent struggles of the final decades of the twentieth century runs quite counter to all the teachings of Buddhism.

In both Thailand and Sri Lanka, however, a minority of monks follow the 'forest tradition', avoiding the towns and dedicating themselves to meditation. Prominent among these was Ajahn Chah, whose followers in Thailand and the West have done much to revive the forest tradition. The American-born Ajahn Sumedho, one of Ajahn Chah's foremost disciples, has helped to found monasteries of that tradition in several parts of the West, most successfully in Britain.

India

In Thailand, Cambodia, India, and Sri Lanka, some Buddhists are playing a significant part in developing forms of peaceful social activism. The late Thai monk, Buddhadasa Bhikkhu, was especially renowned for his efforts to propagate forms of Buddhist practice that address social and political, as well as transcendental, realities. And in India Bahujan Hitay, the social work wing of the Western Buddhist Order, runs educational and medical projects in the new Buddhist community.

Perhaps one of the brightest points of light on the Asian Buddhist scene recently has been the Buddhist revival in India. This was sparked off by Dr B.K.S. Ambedkar, the first Law Minister in independent India. Born a so-called Untouchable, Ambedkar experienced severe oppression at the hands of caste Hindus through-out his formative years. Despite this he was the first Untouchable ever to matriculate, and he went on to gather degrees from London and Columbia Universities, eventually qualifying as a barrister.

Although the Constitution of India, which he himself drafted, made the practice of Untouchability illegal, Ambedkar finally saw that despite all his struggles and campaigns, Hinduism would never grant equal status to the Untouchables, and he decided to seek a new religion for himself and his people. He eventually settled on Buddhism for four reasons: it was Indian in origin, it didn't ennoble poverty, it was based in reason, and it promoted liberty, equality, and fraternity.

In 1956 Ambedkar publicly embraced Buddhism together with 400,000 of his followers. In the next few weeks several hundred thousand more joined them and a movement had begun. Today there are over 10,000,000 new Buddhists in India. Once the lowest of the low, deprived even of the opportunity to practise a religion, the new Indian Buddhists now have a future in a religion that asserts that all can raise themselves up, irrespective of their background, and provides practical guidance in doing so. As a result they show immense reverence and gratitude towards the Buddha and Ambedkar, whose peaceful revolution truly set them free.

But perhaps history will record that the most dramatic event of the twentieth century, so far as Buddhism is concerned, is its taking root in the West, where the technologies of travel and communication, the particularities of the Western psyche, and the fact that all the major Buddhist schools are represented, make for a situation unique in Buddhist history.

Buddhism in the West

In *The Awakening of the West*, the story of the encounter between Buddhism and Western culture, Stephen Batchelor suggests that the Western relationship to Buddhism has been marked by five attitudes: blind indifference, self-righteous rejection, rational knowledge, romantic fantasy, and existential engagement.[28]

This classification can be used in many ways. Most obviously, it details the chronological stages in the encounter between Buddhism and the West, but it can also describe psychological strata within the Western mind: even practising Western Buddhists 'may still entertain romantic notions about enlightenment; attend courses to study Buddhism with rational objectivity from non-Buddhist professors; reject particular ideas as alien features of Asian culture; and be indifferent to aspects of the teachings that, they believe, do not concern them.'[29]

It can also be used to describe current attitudes to Buddhism in the West, where perhaps the majority of people remain blindly indifferent to Buddhism. There are fundamentalists of all hues who self-righteously reject it as well as non-Buddhist academics who specialize in an exclusively rational knowledge of it. Romantic fantasies about Buddhism abound in New Age circles and even in some Buddhist groups, where the first phase of existential engagement is often strongly marked by naivety. Finally, there are experienced Western Buddhist practitioners and teachers, whose existential engagement with the teachings have given rise to significant spiritual insights.

Historically speaking, the period of blind indifference on the part of the West towards Buddhism lasted until the thirteenth century, during which period, with the exception of a few ancient Greeks, Europe had neither knowledge of nor interest in Asian culture. In the middle of that century, however, the threat of a Mongol invasion from the east startled the European powers into an awareness that extended beyond the boundaries of the Mediterranean. Envoys were sent to the court of the Khans and explorers journeyed as far east as Ulan Bator and Peking. Their letters, journals, and reports document the beginnings of the first European knowledge of Buddhism.

From then until the beginning of the eighteenth century the European attitude to Buddhism was almost entirely one of self-righteous rejection, what scant knowledge of it there was leading to its dismissal as a form of heathen idolatry.

The period between the latter part of the eighteenth century and the beginning of the twentieth saw the start of the European 'construction' of Buddhism, for the word 'Buddhism' is a European invention for which no Asian equivalent exists. It came into use for the first time round about the 1830s, as European imperialists strove to make sense of the apparently diverse beliefs and practices present in Asia at the time. The word 'Buddhism' gradually came to be distinguished from other new words (such as 'Hinduism'), and by the 1860s it began to be connected exclusively with the beliefs and practices of people who followed the teachings of the Buddha. What the Europeans began to call Buddhism had, until then, always been known to its various practitioners simply as 'the Dharma'.

Over this same period the Western attitude to Buddhism split in two: one half dealt with Buddhism as a field of rational, scientific knowledge, while the other half turned it into an object of romantic fantasy. This division is perhaps more accurately spoken of as a spectrum.

At one extreme were the early scholars and translators. Towards the centre were artists and philosophers such as Artur Schopenhauer, whose enthusiasm for a partially understood Buddhism in turn infected his followers Richard Wagner and Friedrich Nietzsche. The New England 'Transcendentalists', led by Ralph Waldo Emerson, dabbled in orientalism, and Henry Thoreau translated Eugene Burnouf's translation of the *Lotus Sūtra* into English. In England, Sir Edwin Arnold's great poem *The Light of Asia*, sold in the hundreds of thousands.

At the other end of the spectrum were romantic fantasists such as the early Theosophists, most prominent among whom was Madame Blavatsky, the Russian author of *Isis Unveiled*, and her American partner Colonel Henry Olcott, whose enthusiasm for Buddhism led them, in Ceylon in 1880, to become the first Westerners to undertake the three refuges and five precepts and thus publicly embrace Theravāda Buddhism.

Only at the beginning of the twentieth century did the first small handful of Westerners begin to engage with Buddhism as a path of practice that would address their individual existential concerns, and it was only in the 1960s that the first effective Buddhist spiritual communities began to arise in the West.

Between the 1960s and 1970s most of the Dharma teaching in the West was carried out by Asians, particularly Japanese roshis and Tibetan rimpoches, although a small handful of Westerners, who had travelled to the

East to study Buddhism, had by then returned and were beginning to establish Buddhist groups of their own. Among these were Sangharakshita, the English founder of the Friends of the Western Buddhist Order (FWBO), Robert Aitken Roshi, who founded the Zen Diamond Sangha in Hawaii, and Philip Kapleau Roshi, founder of the Rochester Zen Center in New York State.

During the 1970s representatives from almost every extant Buddhist school in the world arrived in the West where they established urban Buddhist centres, rural retreat centres, or peripatetic teaching programmes. From Tibet there were representatives of the Gelug, Kagyu, Nyingma, and Sakya schools. Japanese Sōtō and Rinzai Zen were well established and one could study Chinese Ch'an, Korean Son, or Vietnamese Thien in many European and American cities, while Burmese, Thai, and Sri Lankan Theravādin teachers offered teachings in their traditions. At the same time, Western forms of Buddhism, such as Sangharakshita's FWBO and Lama Govinda's Arya Maitreya Mandala, were also beginning to take shape.

The academic study of Buddhism also progressed apace. More and more texts were translated into English and other European languages and academic specialists began to render some of the more abstruse points of Buddhist doctrine into terms readily accessible to Western thinkers. Never before in Buddhist history had so much doctrinal material been available at the same time. Buried texts from Central Asia were coming to light which could be compared to later recensions from Tibet,

China, and Japan, as well as earlier material which had survived in Pāli. Buddhologists set to work making comparative studies and the beginning of a scholastically accurate Buddhist 'higher criticism' began to emerge and with it the possibility of sifting the canonical scriptures and dating the different layers of material they contain.

For religions that are founded primarily in belief, such scholastic delving can appear to be a threat, but for Buddhism, founded as it is in experience rather than belief, the results of scholastic analysis can only be welcomed for the clarity they bring to the Buddhist scriptures. By knowing more accurately the chronology of the development of the Buddhist tradition we can come to a clearer understanding of why certain teachings were given when they were, and this can help us to see how we can apply them in our own practice. Thus, increasingly, the academic study of Buddhism has come to be carried out by practising Buddhists whose analysis is motivated as much by a desire to shed light on practice as it is by abstract scholarly interest.

By the mid-1980s a number of Westerners were beginning to assume significant spiritual responsibilities in the Buddhist groups within which they functioned. Several key Asian teachers had died, their places being taken by Western successors, and other teachers began to make plans for handing over their spiritual responsibilities.

Today many hundreds of Western Buddhist teachers carry out their work at some of the thousands of Buddhist centres in Europe, the United States, Australia, New

Zealand, and South Africa. Many of these teachers have come to know one another as personal friends, and the dialogues taking place between – for example, an English bhikkhu practising in the Thai Theravāda tradition and an American woman teaching Sōtō Zen – are helping to expand the Western understanding of what the Buddhist tradition as a whole is about.

Today we stand as heirs to the whole Buddhist tradition and need not identify ourselves exclusively with one or another of the many Asian Buddhist forms. Experienced Western Buddhist practitioners can come to an informed appreciation of the diverse merits of all the different schools and, by empathetically examining the tradition as a whole, can begin to distinguish what is essential from what is peripheral – thus freeing the central, liberative teachings of the Buddha from the weight of later cultural encrustation.

Our brief survey of the history of Buddhism in the West has brought us right up to the present. But what of the future? What will a truly Western form of Buddhism look like? Of course it is too early to say, but a start has been made. We'll therefore conclude by looking at the Buddhist group to which I myself belong. This is the Friends of the Western Buddhist Order, which was founded by an English Buddhist, Sangharakshita, in 1967, and whose primary intention is to translate Buddhism into the local idiom wherever it is practised and to provide supportive conditions for those who wish to practise it.

THE WESTERN BUDDHIST ORDER

In many respects the FWBO is just like any of the other Buddhist groups found in any city in the West today. It offers courses and classes in meditation and Buddhism, celebrates the usual Buddhist festivals, and draws for its teaching on the broad range of Buddhist canonical literature. But in trying to translate the teachings into the local idiom, we have found that we can't just leave it there. In addressing ourselves to issues peculiar to the contemporary Western situation we've had to ask questions such as: What is the relationship of Buddhism to Western culture? How is one's practice of the Dharma affected by economic and political realities? How does a Christian (or even post-Christian) upbringing affect one's attitude to ethics? How can one combine the responsibilities of being a single parent with one's desire to practise the Dharma? These are just a few of the vast complex of issues that arise as a result of the interaction between Buddhism and the social and psychological conditions that prevail in the West today.

As we have seen, the history of Asian Buddhism is largely the history of Buddhist monasticism. Western Buddhism, however, appears to be moving in a different direction. With few exceptions, most of the Buddhist organizations in the West today concern themselves with teaching different varieties of 'lay Buddhism', trying to create some kind of accommodation between the demands of Buddhist practice on the one hand, and those of the modern Western lifestyle on the other.

The FWBO tries to take this one stage further. Questions of lifestyle, we believe, are less important than questions of spiritual commitment. Clearly, a spiritually committed householder is Dharmically better off than a spiritually apathetic monk. But lifestyle inevitably impacts on the possibilities for spiritual practice. It is no easy matter to hold down a regular job, be a parent, keep up a regular meditation practice, attend a Buddhist class each week, and get away for six weeks of retreat each year. We have therefore tried to establish a number of institutions whose primary purpose is to help people lead a viable Buddhist lifestyle today.

At the heart of the FWBO is the Western Buddhist Order itself. This is a new sangha – a spiritual community of men and women who have committed themselves to orienting their lives towards the Three Jewels. This order is neither lay nor monastic. Some of its members choose to be celibate, others not. Some live with their families and hold regular jobs, others live in same-sex residential spiritual communities, work in FWBO Right Livelihood businesses, or teach at FWBO centres. What they all have in common, however, is an commitment to living in accordance with the values embodied in the Three Jewels.

Around this order is a much wider circle of Friends, who have different levels of involvement with the FWBO, from beginners to those training for ordination. Friends might attend just a few FWBO activities a year, or they might live and work alongside members of the order, participating full-time in the FWBO project of finding ways of creating a new Buddhist culture – even a new society.

Addressing the economic imperatives of modern life, we have also tried to develop Right Livelihood businesses. Surplus profits from these help to fund the work of the FWBO. People often work in these businesses on the basis of 'give what you can, take what you need'. Living simply, often communally, remuneration depends on their actual needs, not on the level of responsibility they take.

We cannot progress spiritually by cutting ourselves off from our cultural roots and adopting wholesale a new, Eastern culture. Rather, rooted in Western culture, Buddhists can play a part in the development of the culture itself. For that reason we encourage our members to investigate Western art forms, trying to find what in them resonates with the Dharma. There are several Buddhist Arts Centres associated with FWBO Buddhist centres in the UK. Plays, oratorios, paintings, sculptures, and other works have been produced, and there are regular workshops given over to investigating one or another aspect of the Western cultural tradition.

Around the London Buddhist Centre, the FWBO's largest UK centre, a kind of urban Buddhist village has come into being. There are about a dozen residential communities, several Right Livelihood businesses, a complementary health centre, an arts centre, a Buddhist library, and the Buddhist Centre itself, which runs a programme of around forty different meetings each week at the Centre and elsewhere. Pervading the whole 'village' is an atmosphere of spiritual friendship, for perhaps, above all, this is what people really need to help them grow and develop in today's emotionally alienated environment.

But we don't see ourselves only as providing a friendly supportive matrix for a few people who have a common interest in Buddhism. The world in which we function is in a very sorry state and the task we try to live up to is, in fact, the task of all Buddhists down the ages. The Buddha taught the Dharma not so that a few people might enjoy happier mental states, but for the sake of a world that is being constantly consumed by the flames of greed, hatred, and delusion.

We live in a world of gross material inequality, ecological despoliation, political and psychological oppression, personal isolation, and emotional alienation. And the underlying cause of the devastating waste of human potential that we see all around is nothing but spiritual ignorance. Trapped in worlds of delusive fantasy, driven by the forces of greed, hatred, and spiritual ignorance, we all act again and again in ways which cause ourselves and others to suffer. We act like this because we are fundamentally spiritually ignorant, and we will continue to do so until spiritual truth, the Dharma, informs every dimension of our lives.

Spiritual principles have social implications. Western Buddhists should therefore seek to make the Dharma as widely known as possible, to find ways of living in society that support the individual's practice of the Dharma, and, as a result, to begin to change the world for the better. The task is urgent, for unless Western culture, which is the dominant culture of our age, begins to be informed by values that take us beyond our immense thirst for immediate gratification, it is hard to see how things could not but get very much worse on an over-crowded and under-resourced planet, so much marked by human suffering.

We in the West today have access to enormous riches. Collectively, we command technological and material resources far beyond the dreams of our ancestors. Behind us stands our Western cultural heritage, thousands of years old, rich in goodness, truth, and beauty. Ahead of us lies … what? If we can bring about a marriage, a blending of Buddhism and what is best in Western culture, the future might be glorious indeed.

NOTES AND REFERENCES

1   *Udāna* v.5

2   *Mahāsaccaka Sutta, Majjhima Nikāya* 36, David W. Evans (trans.), *Discourses of Gotama Buddha*, Janus, London 1992, p.110

3   Gwendolyn Bays (trans.), *The Voice of the Buddha (Lalita-vistara Sūtra)*, Dharma Publishing, Berkeley 1983, p.439

4   From Aśvaghoṣa's *Buddhacarita*, in Edward Conze, *Buddhist Scriptures*, Penguin, Harmondsworth 1959, pp.48–9

5   Ibid.

6   *Vinaya Piṭaka, Mahāvagga* I, 5.10

7   op. cit., 10.1

8   *Therīgāthā* 58

9   *Aṅgulimāla Sutta, Majjhima Nikāya* 86

10   *Cūḷadukkhakkhandha Sutta, Majjhima Nikāya* 14

11   *Aṅguttara Nikāya*, i.188. in F.L. Woodward (trans.), *Some Sayings of the Buddha*, OUP, Oxford 1973, p.189

12   'I understood [Krishnamurti] to be saying essentially that the unconditioned acceptance of the conditioned was itself the unconditioned,' Sangharakshita, in a private seminar on chapter 11 of his book, *The Three Jewels*.

13 John Stevens (trans.), *One Robe, One Bowl: The Zen Poetry of Ryokan* Weatherhill, New York and Tokyo 1984, p.50

14 'Burnt Norton' iii

15 From Sangharakshita (trans.), *Dhammapada* 21–5, Windhorse Publications, Birmingham 2001

16 The *Heart Sūtra*, trans. Philip Kapleau, from *Puja: The FWBO Book of Buddhist Devotional Texts*, Windhorse Publications, Birmingham 1999

17 *Dhammapada* op. cit., 184–6

18 Jayasundere (trans.), *Aṅguttara Nikāya* II. 1. vii

19 *Bhikkhus* (Pali), or traditional Buddhist monks, are known as *bhikṣus* (Sanskrit) in Mahāyāna and Vajrayāna contexts.

20 *Saṃyutta Nikāya* v.2

21 Bhikkhu Ñāṇamoli, *The Life of the Buddha*, Buddhist Publication Society, Kandy 1984, pp.114–5

22 See Martin Willson, *Rebirth and the Western Buddhist*, Wisdom Publications, 1987; and Sangharakshita, *Who is the Buddha?* Windhorse Publications, Birmingham 2002

23 *Dhammapada* op. cit., 129–30

24 For a much fuller treatment of these, see Kamalashila, *Meditation: the Buddhist Way of Tranquillity and Insight*, Windhorse Publications, Birmingham 1996

25 Philip Kapleau (ed.), *The Three Pillars of Zen: Teaching, Practice, and Enlightenment*, Anchor Books, New York 1989, pp.61–2

26 Philip B. Yampolsky (ed.), *Selected Writings of Nichiren*, Columbia University Press, New York 1990

27 in e.g. Peter Bishop, *Dreams of Power: Tibetan Buddhism and the Western Imagination*, Athlone Press, London 1993, pp.27,40

28 Stephen Batchelor, *The Awakening of the West: the Encounter of Buddhism and Western Culture*, Parallax Press, Berkeley 1994, p.xi

29 Ibid., p.xii

FURTHER READING

Bodhipaksa, *Wildmind*, Windhorse Publications, Birmingham 2003

Rupert Gethin, *The Foundations of Buddhism*, Oxford University Press, Oxford 1998

Kamalashila, *Meditation: The Buddhist Way of Tranquillity and Insight*, Windhorse Publications, Birmingham 1999

Paramananda, *Change Your Mind*, Windhorse Publications, Birmingham 1996

Saddhaloka, *Encounters With Enlightenment*, Windhorse Publications, Birmingham 2001

Sangharakshita, *What is the Dharma?*, Windhorse Publications, Birmingham 1998

INDEX

F

feeling 49

fire 100

five hindrances 44

five precepts 41, 80ff

forest tradition 115

four antidotes 45

four exertions 43

four noble truths 28

four sights 9ff

friendship 70ff, 127

G

Gandhara 107

gates of the senses 44

generosity 82, 83

globalization 108

God 41

going for refuge 81, 57ff

Govinda, Lama 121

gratitude 105

H

happiness 22, 95

Heart Sūtra 53

Hīnayāna 62, 63

hindrances 44

I

ignorance 86

ill will *see* aversion

impermanence 34, 59

India 108, 116

Indo-China 111

insight 98ff

Insight Meditation Society 115

insubstantiality 34

integration 90, 94, 98

interconnectedness 36, 41

   environment 42

interdependence 41

intoxicants 86

J

Japan 66, 67, 109

K

Kālāmas 23

kalyāṇa mitratā 70

Kannon 65

Kapleau, Philip 121, 130

karma 75

Kisā Gotamī 20

Kondañña 17

Korea 111

Krishnamurti 129

Kuan Yin 65

Kwan Um Zen school 111

L

laity 61

lakṣaṇas see three marks

Lalitavistara Sūtra 12

lama 66

MEDITATING

BY JINANANDA

This is a guide to Buddhist meditation that is in sympathy with modern lifestyle. Accessible and thought-provoking, this books tells you what you need to know to get started with meditation, and keep going through the ups and downs of everyday life. Realistic, witty, and very inspiring.

128 pages
ISBN 1 899579 07 9
£4.99/$7.95/€7.95

VEGETARIANISM

BY BODHIPAKSA

This book explores connections between vegetarianism and the spiritual life.

As a trained vet, Bodhipaksa is well placed to reveal the suffering of animals in the farming industry, and as a practising Buddhist he can identify the ethical consequences of inflicting such suffering. Through the Buddhist teaching of interconnectedness he lays bare the effects our eating habits can have upon us, upon animals, and upon the environment.

He concludes that by becoming vegetarian we can affirm life in a very clear and immediate way, and so experience a greater sense of contentment, harmony, and happiness.

112 pages
ISBN 1 899579 15 x
£6.99/$9.95/€8.95

LIVING TOGETHER

BY SANGHADEVI

Living Together explores the essential ingredients of community living, including friendliness, cooperation, meaningful communication, and mutual vision.

Drawing on her many years in Buddhist communities, Sanghadevi, a widely-respected Buddhist teacher, encourages those who aspire to this lifestyle to engage with the frequent challenges they will encounter and speaks from her experience of the joys of sharing.

112 pages
ISBN 1 899579 50 8
£4.99/$7.95/€7.95

ORDINATION

BY MOKSANANDA

Ordination: a spiritual journey, a noble quest, a lived myth, a rite of passage.

Finding something of true value that evokes our faith and commitment is rare indeed, especially in a time when positive myths are in danger of disappearing. Westerners seeking ordination as Buddhists today are still convinced of the need to commit to the search for spiritual awakening.

Looking at themes such as altruism, purity, loyalty, and courage, and drawing on the example of the Western Buddhist Order, *Ordination* offers some of the mystery and challenge, confusion and joy, that the quest can entail.

Moksananda's conviction and longing – just as strong eighteen years after his own ordination – will echo in many people's hearts as they search for life's meaning.

160 pages
ISBN 1 899579 60 5
£6.99/$10.95/€10.95

The Windhorse symbolizes the energy of the enlightened mind carrying the Three Jewels – the Buddha, the Dharma, and the Sangha – to all sentient beings.

Buddhism is one of the fastest-growing spiritual traditions in the Western world. Throughout its 2,500-year history, it has always succeeded in adapting its mode of expression to suit whatever culture it has encountered.

Windhorse Publications aims to continue this tradition as Buddhism comes to the West. Today's Westerners are heirs to the entire Buddhist tradition, free to draw instruction and inspiration from all the many schools and branches. Windhorse publishes works by authors who not only understand the Buddhist tradition but are also familiar with Western culture and the Western mind.

Manuscripts welcome.

For orders and catalogues vist www.windhorsepublications.com or contact

WINDHORSE PUBLICATIONS	WINDHORSE BOOKS	CONSORTIUM
11 PARK ROAD	PO BOX 574	1045 WESTGATE DRIVE
BIRMINGHAM	NEWTOWN	ST PAUL
B13 8AB	NSW 2042	MN 55114
UK	AUSTRALIA	USA

Windhorse Publications is an arm of the Friends of the Western Buddhist Order, which has more than sixty centres on five continents. Through these centres, members of the Western Buddhist Order offer regular programmes of events for the general public and for more experienced students. These include meditation classes, public talks, study on Buddhist themes and texts, and 'bodywork' classes such as t'ai chi, yoga, and massage. The FWBO also runs several retreat centres and the Karuna Trust, a fund-raising charity that supports social welfare projects in the slums and villages of India.

Many FWBO centres have residential spiritual communities and ethical businesses associated with them. Arts activities are encouraged too, as is the development of strong bonds of friendship between people who share the same ideals. In this way the fwbo is developing a unique approach to Buddhism, not simply as a set of techniques, less still as an exotic cultural interest, but as a creatively directed way of life for people living in the modern world.

If you would like more information about the FWBO visit the website at www.fwbo.org or write to

LONDON BUDDHIST CENTRE	SYDNEY BUDDHIST CENTRE	ARYALOKA
51 ROMAN ROAD	24 ENMORE ROAD	HEARTWOOD CIRCLE
LONDON	SYDNEY	NEWMARKET
E2 OHU	NSW 2042	NH 03857
UK	AUSTRALIA	USA

ALSO FROM
WINDHORSE PUBLICATIONS

THE WHEEL OF LIFE

BY KULANANDA

The Wheel of Life is an ancient symbol of tremendous spiritual significance. It is a graphic representation of the Buddhist understanding of life, a mirror held up to the human heart. Within its depths we see the forces that limit and bind us. We see the happiness and the suffering we create for ourselves. We see the chain of ingrained habits that makes us who we are. But, looking deeper still, we begin to see the way to freedom.

84 pages, illustrated
ISBN 1 899579 30 3
£5.99/$9.95/€9.95

CREATIVE SYMBOLS OF TANTRIC BUDDHISM

BY SANGHARAKSHITA

Tantric Buddhism is concerned with the direct experience of who we are and what we can become. For the Tantra this experience cannot be meditated by concepts, but it can be evoked with the help of symbols.

This is a thorough and informative introduction to:
* The symbolism of colour, mantras, and the mandala of the five Buddhas
* The Tibetan Wheel of Life – a map of our mind and emotions
* Figures of the Tantric tradition – Buddhas, Bodhisattvas, dakinis, and the archetypal guru
* The symbolism of ritual objects and offerings
* Confronting and transforming our fear of crisis situations and death

224 pages, with b&w illustrations
ISBN 1 899579 47 8
£10.99/$19.95/€19.95

A GUIDE TO THE BUDDHIST PATH

BY SANGHARAKSHITA

Which Buddhist teachings really matter? How does one begin to practise them in a systematic way? Without a guide one can easily get dispirited or lost.

In this highly readable anthology a leading Western Buddhist sorts out fact from myth, essence from cultural accident, to reveal the fundamental ideals and teachings of Buddhism. The result is a reliable map of the Buddhist path that anyone can follow.

Sangharakshita is an ideal companion on the path. As founder of a major Western Buddhist movement he has helped thousands of people to make an effective contact with the richness and beauty of the Buddha's teachings.

240 pages, with illustrations
ISBN 1 899579 04 4
£14.99/$24.95/€24.95

BUDDHISM: TOOLS FOR LIVING YOUR LIFE

BY VAJRAGUPTA

A guide for those seeking a meaningful spiritual path while living everyday lives full of families, work, and friends. Vajragupta clearly explains the fundamental Buddhist teachings and guidance on how to apply these to enrich our busy and complex lives.

Personal stories, exercises, reflections, and questions help transform Buddhist practice into more than a set of fine ideals, and make the path of ethics, meditation, and wisdom a tangible part of our lives.

Vajragupta gives a feel for what a Buddhist life might be like for people of various backgrounds and experience. The aim is to make the teachings as accessible and relevant as possible, to present the reader with the tools by which to lead a spiritual life.

ISBN 9781 899579 74 7
£10.99/$16.95/€16.95